School Trip, Love & Trouble

Zimmermann
& Zimmermann

School Trip, Love & Trouble

Aus dem Deutschen
von Michael Turnbull

Thienemann

"Sixty-seven,

sixty-eight, sixty-nine ..." I was counting the stairs. Jenny (that's my mother, but she **freaks out** if I call her Mum, especially in front of other people) and I lived on the fifth floor – without a lift – and on some days I counted in French. Quietly, of course. It would have been really embarrassing to **get caught** doing it.

"Ah, Carlotta, nice to see *you* for a change," interrupted Ms Behringer. Our neighbour! She was all I needed. In my head I quickly counted seventy and tried to give her a smile.

"Which hand do you want?" She stuck out her **hawk**-like face and showed her long teeth. As a baby I would definitely have been frightened of her, but I knew the game by now.

I pretended to think hard and then said, "Left," but with a questioning undertone.

She lowered her eyebrows.

"Right, right," I corrected myself quickly, and then her face **beamed**.

"Good, Carlotta. You're a clever girl," she said **approvingly** and handed over the tenth bag of Gummy Bears that month.

---

to freak out – ausflippen;
to get caught – erwischt werden; hawk – Falke;
to beam – strahlen; approving – anerkennend

"But clean your teeth afterwards," warned Ms Behringer. She had almost closed the door to her flat when she turned round again. "**By the way**," she said, "tell your mother she's not allowed to sing after ten p.m. Especially not **out of tune**."

In the half-light of the stairway she was like a **witch** out of a **fairytale**. I nodded and went slowly up the last **flight of stairs**. Of course I wouldn't say anything to Jenny. She'd had enough stress **recently**, and I knew Ms Behringer's **eternal moaning** and complaints to the housing management wouldn't stop Jenny singing, no matter what time of day.

"I'm an artist," she had explained to the **caretaker** the week before. "An opera singer, if you know what I mean." The guy was impressed, especially when my mother slipped her autograph into his hand and said she might be able to get him and his wife free tickets for the next opera gala.

I unlocked the door to our flat and listened. There was nothing to be heard from the kitchen, which meant that tonight there wouldn't be any guests for dinner going on and on about the latest opera. What a **relief**, I thought and went to look for my mother. She seemed to be in the liv-

---

by the way – übrigens;
out of tune – *hier:* falsch; witch – Hexe;
fairytale – Märchen; flight of stairs – *hier:* Treppenabsatz;
recently – in letzter Zeit; eternal – ewig;
moaning – Klagen; caretaker – Hausmeister;
relief – Erleichterung

ing room. **At any rate**, I could hear her voice. Carefully, I opened the door just a little and **eavesdropped**.

"This time she'll have to go to you," I heard Jenny saying. "**After all,** for the past six months I've arranged my performances so as to be home at least three evenings a week, which has meant a huge **downturn** in my career."

Aha, it was about me, and if I wasn't very much mistaken she was talking to Dad on the phone about which one of them I should live with for the next six months. Since they got divorced I've been living some of the time with Dad and then with Jenny again. My friend Anke is **envious** of me for this. "If you've got **aggro** with your mother, just move in with your father. I wish I had it so easy. I've got my mother and my stupid brothers on my back. And now my mother's boyfriend as well."

Usually, I just smile knowingly at this. Anke doesn't need to know what a pain all this moving is. As soon as I get used to my mother's habits, I have to switch over to my father's.

"Oh, by the way, you could help her out with her Physics," said Jenny, "and her bicycle needs repairing again, and ..."

I shut the door quietly. The list of tasks for my father was endless. I'd seen it recently on the piano and was **pretty** impressed. For an artist,

---

at any rate – auf jeden Fall; to eavesdrop – lauschen;
after all – immerhin, schließlich; downturn – Abflauen;
envious – neidisch; aggro – Ärger, Stress;
pretty – *hier:* ziemlich

Jenny has a **distinct** talent for organisation – at least in terms of things for Dad to do.

Half past two. I took the **remains** of the sandwich Anke had given me out of my school bag. "Emmental again. I can't stand this cheese any more," she had groaned and handed it to me.

I was finishing it off when the door opened.

"Darling! How nice you're back!" My mother beamed at me. "Does this sweatshirt **suit** me? I think the colour combination is very unusual." She twirled around three times and then flopped onto my bed.

I just nodded. She'd probably already forgotten that she'd given me the sweatshirt three weeks ago. But I was **used to** that now. Jenny bought clothes in the young people's section of a department store, put them in my room and after four weeks, at the latest, took them out of my cupboard and wore them herself. But for a while now I've been doing the same. If I fancy something in her cupboard, I wear it. Without asking, of course. I think that's only fair. "Your mother still thinks she's 20," Dad explained to me once when I complained about this habit of hers. "She'll never grow up. It's probably like that with all artists."

There was almost a little **admiration** in his voice when he said it. Dad's a **building engineer** and thinks he's a frustrated artist. But I've never

---

distinct – ausgeprägt; remains – Überreste;
to suit – stehen; to be used to – gewöhnt sein an;
admiration – Bewunderung;
building engineer – Bauingenieur

found out what his line of art is. Perhaps it's his weakness for the theatre.

"So tell me if the sweatshirt suits me," repeated Jenny. "Do you like it? Would you like one, too? What do you think, should I **dye** my hair a different colour? **Copper** perhaps? Or ..."

The telephone rang. Jenny sprang up and opened the door. "Listen, I recorded it today," she whispered, although there was absolutely no reason to whisper. The answering machine was on full volume, and my mother's soprano filled the **entire** flat. "It's Rosetta's aria from ..." but I'll never know which opera it was from.

"Hello, Jenny. I'm afraid I have to cancel my lesson this afternoon," croaked a **hoarse** voice. "Could you lend me the music for a few more days? I'll **be in touch**. Bye!"

"It's Anatol's third cancellation this month," said Jenny, **annoyed**. "You really can't get rich on singing lessons. If only your father would agree to pay a little bit more, I wouldn't have to spend my **precious** afternoons with untalented amateurs. By the way," she hesitated for a moment, "he rang. Your father's **longing to** see you, and he wondered if you'd like to spend the next six months at his place." In a sweeping movement she sat down on my bed again, crossed her legs, and looked at me.

I didn't say anything.

---

to dye – färben; copper – Kupfer; entire – ganz;
hoarse – heiser; to be in touch – *hier:* sich melden;
annoyed – verärgert; precious – kostbar;
to long to do sth. – sich danach sehnen, etw. zu tun

She lowered her head, and I could see the grey **streaks** in her **parting**.

Dad always said I should go easy on Jenny because she was such a sensitive person, but I just couldn't help it. "Are you sure Dad rang and ..."

She beamed at me. "No, now you mention it I remember that I rang him. I read him something out of a research report saying that children **prevent** their parents **from** ageing."

"You could give me that for our Maths teacher," I suggested. "Mr Dannitzki's always saying that after a lesson with us he feels years older. But what's with Dad?"

She nodded cheerfully. "Right, darling. Just take a look at this!" With a triumphant expression she pulled a letter out of her pocket, **smoothed** it **out** carefully and gave it to me.

I only had to see the address to get the message. "Hey, Jenny, that's amazing. When did you hear?"

She laughed happily. "Last week. Just think, if I hadn't changed my agent, I'd never have got such a great offer. An American tour! It's what everyone dreams of. I'd love to have taken you, but when I rang your school, they reacted very strangely and said it wasn't possible. **Compulsory attendance** and things like that."

"Did you really call the school?" I asked.

Jenny nodded. "Of course. We had arranged

---

streak – Strähne; parting – Scheitel;
to prevent from – hindern an;
to smooth out – glatt streichen;
compulsory attendance – Anwesenheitspflicht

for you to live with me for this half of the year, and I thought it didn't really matter whether it was here in the flat or somewhere in America. But your head teacher sees it differently – a typical bureaucrat, if you ask me. Oh well. And now of course I have a terribly **guilty conscience**."

"Don't you think you could just take me with you?" I suggested.

Jenny shook her head. "Your father nearly dropped the **receiver** when I told him. No, but you can live with him, of course, although he's got a new girlfriend, and ..."

"A new one already?" I interrupted her.

"A new one already. And after what he told me about her I'm afraid she isn't right for him either. Your father is a good man, but he has a phenomenal talent for picking the wrong women." She gave a **clucking** laugh. "I've told him a thousand times that he needs someone **down to earth**, without any artistic tendencies. She should be able to do what he can't: **sewing**, cleaning ..."

"Going to parents' evening," I added. I wanted to add a whole lot more, but she interrupted me.

"Carlotta, does that mean you wouldn't be angry with me if I accepted and went on the tour?"

"Of course I wouldn't be angry," I said, feeling very grown up. "You've been dreaming of an

---

guilty conscience – schlechtes Gewissen;
receiver – Hörer; clucking – *hier:* glucksend;
down to earth – bodenständig; to sew – nähen

American tour for years, and I think you should take the **opportunity**."

Jenny flung her arms around my neck. "Carlotta, I'll **grant** you a thousand wishes."

I nodded. "I'll write down the first hundred on a piece of paper, okay? Otherwise you'll forget half of them as usual. Can you help me pack?"

At twenty to eight I rang the bell in Richard-Wagner-Straße. To be on the safe side, I kept my finger on the buzzer for at least ten seconds. I didn't fancy waiting outside for half an hour like last year. That time Dad's new girlfriend had opened the door and said **in astonishment** that she hadn't heard any ringing at all. But this time I seemed to be expected. Before I could say anything, I heard Dad's voice through the **intercom**: "Nice you're here so soon," he said. "Just go into the dining room. I need five more minutes."

I put down my rucksack and sports bag in the hall, took a quick **glance** into the living room and opened the door to the dining room. Dead cool, I thought. Dad, you're the best dad of all time.

White tablecloth, serviettes, candles, red roses, new dishes. Dad had taken **loads of** trouble to welcome me. For a moment I wished I'd taken up Mum's offer of the sweatshirt. But it was too late now. I tried to get rid of the ketchup **stain** on my velour pullover with **spit**, but it didn't work. I

---

opportunity – Gelegenheit; to grant – *hier:* erfüllen; in astonishment – erstaunt; intercom – Sprechanlage; glance – Blick; loads of – jede Menge; stain – Fleck; spit – Spucke

could hear Dad's footsteps on the stairs. **On the spur of the moment** I turned the pullover back to front. The stain was less noticeable on the back, I thought.

Piano music came softly from the living room. "I've got a big surprise for you," called Dad, "but first there's a three-**course** dinner."

It was the right decision to move to Dad's today, I thought **contentedly**. Meals with Dad are a right laugh. He tells me about the firm and I tell him about school, and sometimes I do impressions of the teachers and he says I'll probably become an actress.

"I'm coming," sang Dad and opened the double doors.

I could have cried, I was so touched. Dad had to be really, really pleased to see me. He'd got all dressed up. Good thing my ketchup stain wasn't visible straight away.

He stood in the doorway with his arms open and stared at me.

"Hi, Dad," I said and stood up. Something about the look in his eyes prevented me from flinging my arms around his neck. "Here I am," I said completely unnecessarily.

"Yes," he said after a while. "Here you are. Hey, Carlotta, this evening of all evenings." He grinned in embarrassment. "Well ... How should I put it? If Jenny had at least **hinted** you were coming today." He ran his hand uncertainly

---

on the spur of the moment – spontan;
course – Gang; contented – zufrieden;
to hint – andeuten

through his hair and brought the bits he'd artfully combed over his **balding patch** into complete **disarray**.

The doorbell rang twice. Dad sighed again. Suddenly he looked quite old.

"I'll go to the door," I offered, but he shook his head. "Your hair," I called after him.

"Thank you, thank you," he murmured and straightened it again. Then he closed the door behind him and I was alone.

I was curious, obviously. It had already clicked that this phenomenal effort with the tablecloth, candles, flowers and black suit wasn't for me. Dad only **went to such lengths** for a new girlfriend.

"So-oo," said Dad as he came back in, and he drew out this "so" like a piece of chewing gum. "So-oo."

I stayed sitting down and eyed the new girlfriend. Late twenties – i.e. much younger than Mum – dyed blonde probably, red dress that didn't go with her hair.

"This is Natascha, and this is Carlotta," said Dad, looking pretty unhappy.

Natascha held out her hand to me. I took a piece of white bread from the breadbasket and bit into it demonstratively. Natascha let her hand fall, mumbled something **inaudible** and looked at Dad.

---

balding patch – beginnende Glatze;
disarray – Unordnung;
to go to such lengths – so weit gehen;
inaudible – unhörbar

"Yes, sorry, of course, please sit down. I'll get the starters and then ..."

He disappeared hastily. I almost grinned. Perhaps it hadn't been such a bad idea to suggest to my mother I could surprise Dad that same evening. Although the real reason was that her opera friends were coming for a **rehearsal**, and I wasn't exactly **keen to** hear it.

Natascha had sat herself down on the chair opposite me and was staring at her plate. She was probably **racking her brains** for questions to ask me. She could hardly say, "How you've grown," because it was the first time she'd seen me. A question about school, on the other hand, was always **appropriate**, or about my hobbies or friends or ...

I'd heard it all before. Dad's **last girlfriend but one** always asked me if I enjoyed school. At some point I informed her lightly that I didn't go to school at all, and that all the teachers had screaming fits at the sight of me. "I'm a vampire," I **claimed** and **bared my teeth**. This finally made it clear to her that she wouldn't just be marrying Paul, the owner of a company with 25 employees, but Carlotta as well, his **unruly** daughter, and she gave up.

---

rehearsal – Probe;
to be keen to do sth. – etw. unbedingt tun wollen;
to rack one's brains – sich den Kopf zerbrechen;
appropriate – angemessen;
last girlfriend but one – vorletzte Freundin;
to claim – behaupten; to bare one's teeth – die Zähne fletschen; unruly – renitent, widerspenstig

"What school do you go to?" said Natascha and tried to smile.

"Huh?" I said pointing to my ears.

Dad's new girlfriend **hesitated**, but then she understood. "What school do you go to?" she asked again, but this time much louder.

I looked at her **blankly**.

"What school?" She was almost screaming.

Dad stood in the doorway with a salad bowl. "What's wrong? Why are you shouting, Natascha?

Natascha wanted to say something, but I got in quicker. "Yes, what's wrong with her?" I asked, shaking my head. "She's been shouting like that the whole time."

That evening I was the only one who ate with any appetite. Dad and Natascha just **poked** at their food, but I enjoyed mine. Natascha said goodbye at around half past eight.

"Come tomorrow morning. Carlotta's at school," whispered Dad to her as he helped her into her coat. I heard his exact words.

"Well? Are you satisfied?" he asked as he came back into the dining room. He had shown Natascha to the door, and probably kissed her as well, and now he looked **wrecked**.

I licked my pudding bowl clean.

"Carlotta! Please!"

"At Jenny's you're allowed to," I maintained and almost even wiped my mouth with my

---

to hesitate – zögern; blank – ausdruckslos;
to poke – herumstochern; wrecked – kaputt

sleeve. But I didn't want to overdo things. "The food was excellent, by the way. Did you make everything yourself?"

"Of course I didn't. I got it from a restaurant and heated it up in the microwave," said Dad **indignantly**. "But I don't want to talk about food now, I want to talk about your behaviour. Don't you think you were impossible? After all, Natascha hasn't done anything against you."

Here he was right, for the first time that evening. Although, of course, she would try to get him for herself, just like her **predecessors**. But I had a word or two to say here.

"Believe me, kid," he said, "she's quite different from the others."

"Can she cook? Does she go to parents' evening? Can she bake cakes for next month's school bazaar? Can she replace the **elastic** in my jogging pants?"

I could see quite clearly from his expression that he didn't think she was **capable** of any of these things. **Unsuitable** for a future mother, I thought, but I tried to keep my triumph hidden as far as possible. "What can Natascha do at all? I mean, apart from dying her hair blonde."

Bull's eye! Dad swallowed. "Natascha has very beautiful, naturally dark blonde hair," he said, trying to defend her. "But that's beside the point anyway. She's a great actress and with a bit

---

indignant – entrüstet; ungehalten;
predecessor – Vorgänger/-in; elastic – Gummiband;
to be capable of – fähig sein zu;
unsuitable – unpassend; Bull's eye! – Volltreffer!

of luck she'll get the lead in Nora soon. It's a play by Ibsen and ..."

"Another actress," I sighed.

He gathered up the plates and carried them into the kitchen. I stuffed the remains of the potato gratin into my mouth. No thanks, I'd had enough of Dad's actresses, who were all so terribly talented but **were** never **up to** one **crucial** role: Mum.

There was a loud clatter from the kitchen. "It was just the plates," called Dad. "No damage. But believe me, Natascha's different. Please give her a chance!"

---

to be up to sth. – geeignet sein;
crucial – entscheidend

I lay awake

half the night thinking **evil** thoughts. It wasn't that I **begrudged** Dad a new girlfriend. He could even marry her if he wanted to. But not over my head, because it affected me after all. It was a good thing I'd come here in time to prevent a disaster called Natascha. Natascha! What kind of a name was that? But it was probably just her stage name, and she was really called Angelika or Anneliese or something. I **giggled** quietly and fell asleep.

The alarm clock woke me up at half past seven. At first I wanted to draw attention to myself loudly, but then I remembered yesterday evening and tiptoed downstairs. Dad still seemed to be asleep.

I found the telephone under a flowery **silk** shawl, which I held up with a **frown**. Red roses on a black background. Natascha all over. I stuffed the shawl into the umbrella stand, right to the bottom.

Then I dialled my school's number. I knew it **by heart** because I'd rung them so often. The first time was around two years **previously**, when I

---

evil – böse; to begrudge – missgönnen;
to giggle – kichern; silk – Seide; frown – Stirnrunzeln;
by heart – auswendig; previously – zuvor

had crawled into Jenny's room one morning with a temperature of at least 40 degrees and asked her to excuse me from school. But she had just rolled over with a **yawn** and said, "Darling, ring them yourself. You want to become independent after all." When the school secretary asked me who she was speaking to, I had answered, "My mother."

But I didn't make mistakes like that any more. I rattled off my speech like an expert. "This is Jenny Bergmann. Good morning. I'd like to excuse my daughter Carlotta because of **nausea**. Goodbye." I hung up.

Meanwhile Dad was in the bathroom. Of course he **assumed** his daughter had gone to school already. "Will you be all right on your own in the morning?" he had asked the evening before, and I had assured him he didn't have to worry about anything. To be on the safe side I took my jacket out of the wardrobe and slipped back into my room. No one would think I was still at home.

But Dad didn't quite trust me. I just had time to pull the **duvet** over my head when he looked into my room at half past eight. It was lucky I hadn't opened the shutters yet and he didn't take a closer look. Shortly afterwards the doorbell rang twice and I knew it would soon be time for my big entrance.

I wanted them to think they were safe for a while, so I waited almost three quarters of an

---

yawn – Gähnen; nausea – Übelkeit;
to assume – annehmen; duvet – Bettdecke

hour before marching into the living room in my pyjamas, with a thick woollen scarf around my neck. Dad and his new girlfriend were sitting **suspiciously** close together on the sofa and had either been **smooching** or talking about me. At any rate, they jumped up guiltily when they saw my long-suffering face in the doorway.

"But you're at school," said Dad, staring at me, "aren't you?"

"And you're at the office," I **rejoined**, "aren't you?"

"Carlotta, I always have Wednesday mornings off. It's been that way for years and you know it," said Dad in self-justification. "But I can't imagine that you have a regular morning off school now."

"I **feel rotten**," I said, which was even true. Well, all right, I was fine physically, but I hated the thing with Natascha. So I did feel rotten.

Natascha gave me a **sympathetic** look. "Have you got a temperature?"

I decided to ignore this question. She'd probably stick a thermometer into my **gob**, diagnose a perfectly normal temperature and pack me off to school in person.

"So tell us what's wrong!" Dad seemed pretty annoyed.

I made a face. "No idea what's wrong. Am I a doctor? But I feel rotten. Perhaps it's an upset

---

suspicious – verdächtig;
to smooch – knutschen, schmusen; to rejoin – erwidern;
to feel rotten – sich mies fühlen;
sympathetic – mitfühlend; gob – Mund

stomach. It could be from the food yesterday evening."

Dad nodded at Natascha. "I wouldn't be surprised, **considering** how much my beloved daughter stuffed into herself last night. So go back to bed, Carlotta. We have things to discuss here."

I'd rather have sat down with them on the sofa, but I didn't want to overdo things. I walked to the door with a pained expression. "I see, you want to be alone," I said in a deathly murmur.

"No, of course we don't," lied Natascha. "You know what, I'll cook you something nice later. I can make something light that'll be sure to agree with you. What do you **fancy**?"

Aha, Dad had already given Natascha her instructions. You'll only win Carlotta's heart if you give her the 'caring-mum' number. I wouldn't fall for it, of course, but it wouldn't **do** her any **harm** to make the effort.

"I'll think about it," I announced **graciously** and retired to my room.

A little while later Natascha put her head round the door. She had knocked quietly and waited for a moment. This enabled me to hide my Walkman quickly under the duvet. I opened my eyes and blinked.

"Better?" she asked.

I shook my head.

"Have you thought about what I could make you to eat?"

---

to consider – bedenken; to fancy – Lust auf etw. haben; to do harm – schaden; gracious – gnädig

I nodded.

"Well?" Natascha smiled.

I was gradually beginning to admire her. She really must be a good actress because she'd certainly have rather given me **a slap round the face**.

Dad appeared in the doorway – he probably wanted to rush to his girlfriend's aid, in case his daughter went wild and suddenly revealed her claws – but Natascha just pushed him aside.

"Well?" she asked again **gently**.

"Home-made noodles with thick chocolate sauce," I said. "That's what my mother always makes when I'm ill."

"Noodles with chocolate sauce?" asked Natascha.

"Home-made noodles with thick chocolate sauce," I corrected her. Then I turned myself to the wall, as I could hardly **suppress** my giggles.

"And that's what your mother always makes?" Natascha had sat down on the edge of my bed and was stroking my hair. A pity she **was after** Dad, or I'd have found her quite nice. But we were opponents, and the fight was on.

"Yes," I **lied** and had to really pull myself together so as not to **burst out** laughing. I put a bit more tragedy into my voice. "My mother makes the best home-made noodles with thick chocolate sauce you can imagine."

---

a slap around the face – eine Ohrfeige;
gentle – sanft; to suppress – unterdrücken;
to be after sb. – hinter jmdm. her sei; to lie – schwindeln;
to burst out – herausplatzen

Natascha didn't say another word. She just sat on my bed without moving until Dad called to her impatiently from downstairs.

She had hardly left the room when I took out my Walkman again and enjoyed the feeling of having given her a ton of problems.

"Would our princess like to take her royal **repast** in bed or in the dining room?" Dad **enquired** around midday. He looked friendly enough, but I could see he was about to flip. He'd probably imagined quite a different morning with Natascha.

I stretched my limbs. "I'm feeling a little better. I'll come down."

I put on the pullover with the ketchup stain again, but this time the right way round. Natascha might as well see how **neglected** I was in this household.

She seemed a bit stressed and uncertain as I entered the dining room. But still, there was a bowl full of noodles on the table and next to it, in a glass carafe, the chocolate sauce.

"Are the noodles home made?" I asked. "And the sauce seems a bit thin."

Dad had gone **pale**. "Carlotta," he said in a really **weird** voice, "I **forbade** Natascha to spend half the morning in the kitchen making noodles. These are out of a packet and you've always liked them. And apart from that, what makes you

---

repast – Mahl; to enquire – anfragen;
to neglect – vernachlässigen; pale – blass;
weird – eigenartig; to forbid – verbieten

think your mother would ever cook such a thing?"

I just ignored this question. "Natascha's stuff doesn't look too bad," I said **patronisingly** and smiled at her. What did Dad want? He'd said I should give Natascha a chance. This was her chance.

I **piled** a mountain of noodles onto my plate and poured chocolate sauce all over them.

Dad shook his head **decisively** and muttered something about not eating and having a serious word with me that evening. Before he could continue, the phone rang and he jumped up. "Enjoy your food, you two," he said, slamming the door behind him. He probably thanked the caller a thousand times for rescuing him from the meal.

Meanwhile Natascha had placed around twenty noodles on her plate. She hesitated, and I watched her out of the corner of my eye. With a **disgusted** expression she poured the sauce over them. Respect, I thought.

"Bon appetit, Natascha," I said and forked up **a couple of** noodles from the edge of my plate where there wasn't much sauce.

Natascha had taken her first nibble. "Well? How do you like the sweet noodles," I asked.

She paused. "They take a bit of getting used to."

She bravely went on eating. I poured myself a

---

patronising – gönnerhaft; to pile – häufen;
decisive – bestimmt; disgusted – angewidert;
a couple of – einige

glass of mineral water and drank it slowly. Then I stood up.

"Don't you like it?" asked Natascha. "You've hardly touched it."

"I think it's great that you went to so much trouble," I said, "but I still feel quite weak, you know. I think I should go back to bed."

In the hall I ran straight into Dad's outstretched arms. "My beloved daughter," he said, although it didn't sound as if he meant it, "if you don't **alter** your behaviour, you'll be in big trouble, believe me."

I nodded twice. That's the best way to deal with long speeches.

But this time he really seemed to be serious. "I know you're ..."

On the spur of the moment I held my hand to my mouth and rolled my eyes.

"There's a **bucket** in the bathroom," Dad called after me as I ran upstairs.

He'd hardly disappeared into the dining room when I slipped back down again and made myself a pile of sausage sandwiches. I was mega hungry and, who knows, perhaps Dad would get it into his head to serve noodles and chocolate sauce again that evening – as a sort of educational measure.

Upstairs in my room I switched on the **portable telly** I'd taken from Dad's bedroom and decided to have a **cosy** afternoon.

A little later I heard Dad coming up the stairs.

---

to alter – ändern; bucket – Eimer;
portable – tragbar; telly – Fernseher; cosy – gemütlich

I just had enough time to throw the duvet over the television and get back onto the bed before he came into the room and gave me a searching look.

"Are you feeling better?" he wanted to know.

For a moment I wondered whether I should still look as if I was suffering terribly. But here there was the danger of him covering me with the duvet and discovering the television.

"No, no, I'm much better," I asserted hastily.

Dad seemed happy. "There you see, it's not so bad. **Hang on**, I'll bring you the television from my bedroom, just this once."

"Oh no! I don't feel *that* well yet," I said weakly.

Dad looked at me in astonishment. "Do you think we can leave you alone?" "Yes, of course. I'll be all right," I **reassured** him.

He bent down, gave me a kiss on the forehead and waved goodbye as he went out.

Minutes later I was standing behind the curtains watching the two of them going side by side through the garden gate. Natascha placed her hand on Dad's arm for a moment. On the street he turned round and looked up to me. Poor Dad. His hair was really thinning out. Next year he'd be 50. Was it worth getting married at all at that age? Or was it better to look around for a good **geriatric nurse**?

---

to hang on – einen Augenblick warten;
to reassure – versichern; geriatric nurse – Altenpflegerin

"Why didn't you tell me you were living at your dad's again? I've been trying to reach you the whole afternoon, and the answering machine's on the whole time at your mum's place. And then you have to listen to all that singing. Do you know what it **reminds me of**?" My mate Anke made a dramatic pause. "Don't be annoyed, but we once had a cat, and when you **trod** on its tail it yowled in the same way."

"Oh yeah?" I said. "Very funny."

"Are you angry?"

"Angry? No, why should I be angry?" If she was looking for a fight, I was the wrong person today. My enemy was Natascha, and I wanted to concentrate all my energy on her.

"Oh well, it doesn't matter anyway. Pity you weren't at school. We nearly **went ballistic**. They just can't do that to us. All the planning and then it's cancelled."

"What do you mean? What's been cancelled?"

"The school trip to Berlin. Ms Reiser broke her leg yesterday during Sports and she's in hospital. And none of the other teachers are prepared to go to Berlin with us. Can you imagine, the trip's **off**! And I was looking forward to Berlin so much." Anke sniffed loudly and clearly.

She had moved to our town from Hamburg two years ago, and would sometimes **show off** her city past. Anke, of course, would have preferred

---

to remind sb. of sth. – jmdn. an etw. erinnern;
to tread – treten; to go ballistic – ausrasten;
to be off – abgesagt sein;
to show off – angeben mit

the class to go to Hamburg, but Berlin **narrowly** won the vote. "Okay, Berlin is acceptable, too," she had declared **magnanimously**. "The main thing is to get a breath of city air."

"Why don't you say something? Don't you get it? Berlin is cancelled!" repeated Anke.

I murmured something about it being **outrageous**, but, actually, it fitted in quite well. At least now I could keep an eye on Dad and his new girlfriend. Ten days were a long time, and who knows, Natascha might have moved in by then.

"It's even worse," said Anke indignantly. "The head teacher knows the **wardens** of a hostel in a village in **Saxony** and he got some places **at short notice**, so we're going to go to Erdmannsweiler instead."

"Erdmannsweiler?"

"Erdmannsweiler! They probably have nothing but clean air and a few sheep and goats. You can forget shopping and discos and everything."

"Shit," I said. I **was gutted**. Three years ago our class had been to a hostel in a mountain village and we almost died of boredom. It would be exactly the same in Erdmannsweiler, I was sure of it.

"Are you still there?" asked Anke.

"Yeah. I'm just wondering what we can do about it. What if we all just refused to go?"

---

narrowly – knapp; magnanimous – großmütig;
outrageous – unerhört, skandalös;
warden – Herbergsleiter/-in; Saxony – Sachsen;
at short notice – kurzfristig;
to be gutted – bitter enttäuscht sein

"The others think Erdmannsweiler is fine. At least they pretend to. You know Tina! She started **sucking up to** everyone straight away and said Erdmannsweiler would be full of surprises." Anke gave a bitter **chuckle**. "Surprises. Don't make me laugh."

"Hey, Anke, we were so looking forward to Berlin. I'm sure we'll come up with something to prevent Erdmannsweiler. For example we could ..."

"I'm **in such a state**," Anke interrupted, " that I haven't told you Danni's coming, too."

"Danni?" I repeated. "I thought our Maths teacher refused to go on school trips. Didn't he say so again last year?"

"Yes, but if the head teacher asks him to ... At any rate, he's coming with us to Saxony. Now we just need a woman supervisor as well. But none of the female teachers in our school can come, and Danni's wife doesn't want to and ..."

"But that's our chance," I said. "The school can't find anyone, so we'll stay at home until Ms Reiser is better and then go to Berlin."

"That would be fine," sighed my friend, "but Danni says we should ask at home if a mother would be prepared to come with us. Tina said straight away that her mother might enjoy it."

"No way," I said.

Anke agreed with me that Erdmannsweiler with Tina *and* her mother would be worse than anything, but unfortunately, we couldn't think of

---

to suck up to sb. – sich bei jmdm. einschleimen; chuckle – Kichern; to be in a state – sich aufregen

a way to prevent the **looming** disaster. We ended our phone call in frustration.

To make sure that Anke had understood everything correctly, I rang up Stefanie. You can **rely on** her 100 percent. She's the only one in our class who always knows what homework was set and when the next test is.

"What do you think of Erdmannsweiler?" I asked.

Stefanie laughed. "Hostels are always fun, and if we can't have Berlin, we'll just take Erdmannsweiler. Mr Dannitzki only has three or four days free, because he has to go on a course, but I think that's better than nothing. I hope he can find someone to come with us."

I decided to say nothing. What with her **twin bro** and two younger **siblings**, Stefanie is always glad to get away.

We agreed that it would probably be quite difficult to find a woman to accompany us at such short notice, and then she gave me that day's Maths homework. "Thanks, Stefanie," I said. "What would I do without you?"

Over the following days Anke and I **feverishly** discussed how to prevent the trip to Saxony, but it seemed hopeless. Tina's mother was 50 percent prepared to come with us, as Tina proudly announced, and apparently wanted to decide on Friday.

---

looming – drohend; to rely on – sich verlassen auf; twin bro – Zwillingsbruder; siblings – Geschwister; feverish – fieberhaft

I didn't give anything away at home. I was even extra nice to Dad. And he pulled himself together, let me win at cards, didn't say a word about Natascha or even ring her. At least not when I was there. He was probably **comforting** himself with the fact that he'd soon **be rid of** me for ten days.

"Do you need anything for your school trip?" he asked at Thursday breakfast. "Shoes, umbrella, travel bag or anything?"

"Ah, the school trip." I carefully finished **spreading** my **roll**. I'd actually wanted to wait until Saturday evening to tell him, but now I had no choice. I looked straight at him. "It's been messed up. We wanted to go to Berlin with our class teacher, Ms Reiser, and just think ..."

He looked impatiently at his watch. "So, how much money do you need?"

I shook my head indignantly. "I don't need any money. The trip's probably off."

Dad replaced his cup with a clatter, spilling his coffee as he did so, but he didn't seem to notice. "Wait a second, Carlotta. This means you're not going to Berlin?"

I nodded. I was almost sorry for him. "Mr Dannitzki hasn't been able to find a woman to go with us yet, so we're not going to Erdmannsweiler either."

Ten minutes later he had got the picture. At

---

to comfort – trösten;
to be rid of sb. – jmdn. los sein;
to spread – bestreichen;
roll – Brötchen

first he **got** all **worked up** about teachers who are paid from his **taxes** but aren't prepared to go on a school trip with his daughter. Then he calmed down. "Perhaps your Maths teacher will find someone after all," he said optimistically. "Some mother or other who hasn't got enough housework could do a good **deed** and go with you."

I promised to suggest this to Mr Dannitzki in the first lesson. "Or he could ask at the job centre. For heaven's sake, there are so many unemployed people he's **bound to** find someone to go with you to Erdmannshofen."

"Erdmannsweiler," I corrected him. "I'll tell Mr Dannitzki everything you said."

I was just taking my bike out of the garage to go to school when I had *the* idea. Why hadn't I thought of it before? Of course, this was our only chance to prevent Erdmannsweiler! Anke would be grateful to me **for yonks**. And at the same time I could make it clear to Dad that Natascha simply wasn't suitable as a future mother.

I looked at my watch. If I was in luck, I'd still catch Dad. I'd miss the first lesson, but this was a **sacrifice** I had to make.

"Are you still here? Have you forgotten something?" Dad was standing in the hall rubbing at a stain on his trousers.

"I've just thought of something, Dad," I said

---

to get worked up – sich aufregen
tax – Steuer; deed – Tat;
to be bound to do sth. – etw. sicherlich tun;
for yonks – jahrelang; sacrifice – Opfer

and tried not to **smirk**. "You know the school trip to Saxony I told you about just now. I've got an idea ..."

Dad pointed to his trouser leg. "Can you still see the stain?"

I shook my head. "All we need is a woman to come with us. If ..."

The phone rang and Dad shook his head. "I've no time at the moment, darling. That's bound to be Olemöller not knowing what to do yet again. It's chaos in the firm at the moment. He should try and work things out for himself."

Dad reached for his **briefcase**. I had to hurry, that was clear.

"I thought perhaps Natascha could come with us."

The telephone fell silent. Dad leaned against the **shoe cabinet** and looked at me questioningly. "You can't be serious."

"Yes, I am. You said I should give her a chance. I mean, if she came with us to Erdmannsweiler we might get on really well together and ..."

He gave a short laugh. "Natascha isn't a nanny. I can't possibly ask her to **supervise** a school trip. She's an artist, and that's enough. I hardly think she could do it, or even want to, educational **stuff** like that. That's what teachers are for, aren't they?"

"Well, it was just a question," I said, trying hard not to show my satisfaction. *The first* **seeds**

---

to smirk – grinsen; briefcase – Aktentasche;
shoe cabinet – Schuhschrank;
to supervise – beaufsichtigen; stuff – Zeug; seed – Same

of doubt were **sown**, I had recently read somewhere. **Aptly** put. Dad would gradually come to see how unsuitable Natascha was to be my future mother.

"But you could at least ask her."

He rummaged in his briefcase and nodded **absent-mindedly**. "Yes, yes, if I get the opportunity."

Now for the next move.

The chance came in the Maths lesson.

"The decision has to be taken by this evening," said Danni, looking **severely** at Tina. "So, what about your mother? She said she'd ring me and ..."

"The best thing would be to ring her after the lesson. She's 85 percent sure of coming," stuttered Tina. She was **blushing**. "The other 25 percent ..."

"Tina! Didn't you get an A in Maths last year?" Mr Dannitzki shook his head **in bewilderment**.

Tina didn't say another word.

That was my chance. I put up my hand. "Mr Dannitzki, there's another possibility. My father wants to ask a friend, and she'd be able to come for sure. I'll give you her phone number after the lesson, and you could ring her this afternoon. I'm sure it'll be a great trip. And Tina can let her mother know she doesn't have to come."

Everyone turned to look at me, all talking at once. Anke gave me a shocked look. "I thought

---

to sow – säen; apt – passend;
absent-minded – abwesend; severe – ernst;
to blush – rot werden; in bewilderment – verwundert

you wanted to prevent Erdmannsweiler?" she **riled**.

"That's what I'm doing," I whispered back. "Just leave it to me."

"So how are you going to do it?" asked Anke in the break.

I laughed. "I've had a brilliant idea. Have I told you about my father's new girlfriend? About Natascha?"

She shook her head irritably and unpacked her sandwiches. "This cheese again. Do you want it?"

I nodded, took a large bite and pulled Anke to one side. I didn't want anyone else to hear what I was about to say.

"Natascha is my father's new girlfriend. She doesn't **have a clue** about this school trip. Danni's fed up with Tina's mother, he rings Natascha, but she can't leave in the middle of the theatre season, and ..."

"What if they find out you've set up the whole thing?"

"I only said that my father wanted to talk to her about the trip. And that's what he promised me, too. But I'm pretty sure that Danni will **call off** Erdmannsweiler this evening."

I did feel a bit **uneasy**, though. Dad would probably give me a lot of aggro if he found out, but I had to **bite the bullet**.

---

to rile – sich ärgern;
to not have a clue – keine Ahnung haben;
to call off – absagen; uneasy – unbehaglich;
to bite the bullet – in den sauren Apfel beißen

Anke **nudged** me in the ribs. "If it works, I'll take you to the wickedest disco in Berlin."

I had Sports in the afternoon, and it was half past five when I got home. Dad was nowhere to be seen, which was the best thing for the moment. Perhaps Natascha had rung him up straight after talking to Danni and told him everything.

I'll show Dad I only mean well, I thought. Perhaps freshly cleaned windows would make him happy. But knowing my luck, he wouldn't even notice. I decided to make chocolate **blancmange** and leave most of it for him, as a sort of **consolation**. And I also **resolved** to look through the marriage ads for a **proper** wife for him.

I had just poured the blancmange into a glass bowl when I heard the front door opening.

"Carlotta? Are you there?" called Dad.

"I'm in the kitchen," I replied. "I've got a surprise for you."

He opened the kitchen door and laughed. "I've got a surprise for you, too." Natascha was standing behind him, looking quite jolly. I thought that describing Natascha as a surprise was going way too far.

"Have you made that delicious blancmange?" she asked. "With **almonds**?"

I nodded. I would never in my whole life have admitted that the **lumps** she was pointing to weren't almonds.

---

to nudge – stoßen; blancmange – Pudding;
consolation – Trost; to resolve – beschließen;
proper – geeignet; almond – Mandel; lump – Klümpchen

"Great," said Natascha **appreciatively**. "My blancmange always has lumps in it. Can we have some now?"

The two of them finished the lot, straight from the bowl. I couldn't eat a thing. Why didn't Natascha say anything about Danni's phone call? I'd like to have asked her, but I didn't **have the bottle**. Perhaps Danni hadn't rung her at all?

Once the bowl was empty, Natascha said goodbye. She had such a lot to do, she told me, and I replied coldly, "I didn't ask you to stay longer."

"Don't you want to stay, Natascha, until I've told Carlotta everything?" said Dad, **sticking his oar in** with a **reproachful** look at me.

But she waved him off. "I think it's better to leave the two of you alone."

Dad saw her to the door. I scraped the remains of the blancmange out of the bowl and was still pretty sure Danni had cancelled the school trip.

Ten minutes later Dad came back into the living room. He'd probably been **snogging** with Natascha the whole time.

"You've got lipstick on your face," I **maintained**. If Dad had been paying attention, he'd have said that wasn't true because Natascha never wore lipstick. But he didn't **catch on**, and

---

appreciative – dankbar;
to not have the bottle – nicht den Mut haben;
to stick one's oar in – sich einmischen;
reproachful – vorwurfsvoll; to snog – knutschen;
to maintain – behaupten; to catch on – kapieren

instead wiped his face absent-mindedly with a handkerchief.

"And anyway, I thought you had a surprise for me," I said. "Or was that supposed to be Natascha?"

Dad laughed. "Oh, the surprise, yeah, right. Look, let's drink to your school trip with a glass of apple juice."

"It's probably been cancelled," I explained. "I'll be here and can look after you."

He shook his head and poured out the apple juice. "Cheers! To your school trip. Shorter than planned, but better than nothing. The woman supervisor has been found. Natascha's making the **supreme** sacrifice."

"But this morning you said that ..."

"To be honest I didn't think Natascha would go. But when she rang up this morning, she was quite taken with the idea and went straight round to Mr Dannitzki to discuss everything with him. He's something, I tell you." Dad was laughing so much he **spilled** his apple juice. "Just imagine, he pretended to know that Natascha was going already. At least that was her impression. **Is** the guy **psychic**? So, what have you got to say?"

At first I didn't say a thing. I was speechless. I had to think through the new situation. Natascha as supervisor – mega **cringe**! And what would Anke say? I'd totally **messed up** Berlin.

Dad sat down in an armchair and looked at me

---

supreme – extrem groß; to spill – verschütten;
to be psychic – hellsehen können; cringe – Peinlichkeit;
to mess sth. up – etw. vermasseln

expectantly. "Say something," he demanded. "It was your idea to ask Natascha after all. I don't understand why you aren't pleased."

"Well, I don't know if it's so good," I said slowly. "I mean, Natascha can't do anything. I mean, educational stuff."

Dad tried hard to stay friendly. He wandered up and down between the door and the window. "Natascha doesn't have to do anything more than take a look at you girls once in a while and hold your hands if you have any problems. Your teacher's responsible for everything else."

"But what about the theatre?" I objected. "I mean, can she just go away in the middle of the season?"

"Yes, she can." Dad sounded resolute. "The situation in the theatre here is difficult. There are too many actors and not enough roles. Natascha hasn't got an engagement at the moment, so she can go away. *Tu comprends*?"

I understood.

In my room I lay down on the bed and thought about things. The trip to Saxony would take place, and Natascha would come with us. Too embarrassing! And someone who could in all seriousness make noodles with chocolate sauce, and even eat it, was bound to create even more embarrassment.

Of course Natascha would keep an eye on me more than anyone else. I'd be under **parental**

---

parental – elterlich

control, so to speak, and in front to the whole class, too. It wasn't what I'd planned.

Anke had to help me.

I only had a single comfort. Dad and Natascha wouldn't see each other for a few days. With this thought I fell asleep.

Your friend

Anke phoned three times!!! read the note Dad had left for me on the breakfast table. There wasn't a **trace** of him in the whole house. He was probably at Natascha's. But at least he'd thought to put out a roll and my favourite **jam**.

I was spreading a thick **layer** of it when the phone rang.

"Dannitzki called all the parents yesterday and said that Erdmannsweiler was on!" Anke was in a state. "Hey, Carlotta, your plan wasn't bad, but it's gone badly wrong. You know this means we're going to Erdmannsweiler, don't you. I could **weep**. Have you taken a close look at Danni's list? Hiking boots, rucksack, **plasters** in case we get **blisters**, and stuff like that." There was an **exhausted** silence. "What are we going to do now?"

"Sorry I **botched** it," I said **sheepishly**. "But I was so sure Natascha wouldn't come with us. Can you imagine how awful this is for me? She'll probably want to play mother."

---

trace – Spur; layer – Schicht; jam – Marmelade;
to weep – heulen; plaster – Pflaster; blister – Blase;
exhausted – erschöpft; to botch – verbocken;
sheepish – kleinlaut

Anke gave me a sympathetic "Poor thing."

"She probably wants to test my reactions for when she moves in here," I added.

"What? Does she want to marry your father?"

"Probably. Actually, I'm pretty sure she does. But there's an **obstacle**, and that's me. They might ask me what *I* think about it."

"You're right," said Anke **supportively**. "You're the person it **affects** most after all. What does Natascha look like anyway? I mean, is she pretty?"

"Pretty?" I thought for a moment. "No, I don't think you could say that. She's all artificial. False **eyelashes** and ..."

"Silicon breasts?" giggled Anke. "That's true for most actresses. Don't tell me your father hasn't noticed."

"My mother always says that men never notice anything. And that **applies** to my father one hundred percent. I really have to protect him from Natascha. She has to see that she can't get Dad."

"I'll help you," promised Anke. "Perhaps Erdmannsweiler won't be so boring after all."

We were all to meet at the station on Sunday evening a little after nine. Of course Mr Dannitzki would have preferred to travel during the day. "Then at least we'd see something of the landscape." But this way we saved a night in the hostel. "Please be punctual. Anyone late stays at

---

obstacle – Hindernis; supportive – unterstützend;
to affect – betreffen; eyelashes – Wimpern;
to apply to sb. – auf jmdn. zutreffen

home," he had threatened, and murmured that it was easier to look after a sack of **fleas** than a class of girls.

"I'm so glad you're coming with us, Ms Lewin," he said to Natascha without a word about her being two minutes late. "We're in good time. The train arrives in 15 minutes."

"So why did we have to come so early?" complained Andrea, but **in an undertone**.

Dannitzki took a piece of paper out of his beige **windcheater** and raised his voice to read aloud from it. "It's marvellous of Ms Lewin to enable the class to spend some unforgettable days in the heart of Saxony. And I think that's worth a round of applause."

His wife had probably dictated the text. Then he actually clapped his hands, and a few **creeps** copied him. Natascha was embarrassed, you could tell, but I didn't have **a scrap of sympathy** for her. No one had asked her to come, least of all me.

"Apart from that," added Danni," I'm sure you will understand that we won't be able to carry out the programme intended for Berlin in Erdmannsweiler, but I have planned some very nice walks, and perhaps you can amuse yourselves now and then as well. You're old enough after all."

"Walks," I heard someone **groan** behind me.

---

flea – Floh; in an undertone – leise;
windcheater – Windjacke; creep – *hier:* Schleimer;
not a scrap of – kein bisschen; sympathy – Mitleid;
to groan – stöhnen

"Why do teachers like walking so much? I hate going for walks."

Our train was late, of course. Most of the parents had already left. Only Stefanie's family was still standing with us on the platform.

"Hey look, poor thing," I said to Anke. "It's as if she was going on a world tour. They've probably even brought handkerchiefs to wave with."

I had come to the station on my own. Dad didn't want to stand there between me and Natascha. At any rate, he said he hated stations and would I **mind** taking a taxi? And he thought waving on platforms was silly, and probably I did, too. I nodded. He put an envelope into my hand. "For the taxi," he said, "and the rest is extra pocket money. I don't want to be **stingy** if you're going on a school trip."

No, he definitely wasn't stingy. But perhaps it had been a mistake to take the money. A **bribe**, I thought, and eyed Natascha, who was still standing beside Mr Dannitzki looking totally insecure. If I had insisted on Dad coming to the station, he would have had to choose between us. And I hardly think he would have kissed Natascha goodbye in front of everyone. He probably wouldn't even have **dared** to wave to her. Pity I didn't think of that before, I thought, annoyed with myself.

The train had only just come in when the fight for the best seats began. Dannitzki had been able to reserve a whole carriage for us at short

---

to mind – etw. dagegen haben; stingy – geizig; bribe – Bestechungsgeld; to dare – wagen

notice, but, of course, everyone wanted to sit with their friends.

"First one in saves the seats," Anke had said to me.

"And not in a **compartment** with Danni or Natascha," I added.

While most of the class waited like good girls in front of carriage seven until the passengers had got off, I ran to the next-but-one carriage and was able to get on easily. In the train I ran back and sat down in the second compartment of our carriage and felt quite pleased with myself. Half a minute later an older couple **flung open** the door. "I'm sorry," I said politely, "all these seats are occupied."

"Of course they are," **growled** the man. "We reserved them. Please get up. The rest of the seats are for our grandchildren." An irritated mother **shoved** four small children into the compartment and said she'd have to get off quickly because the train was leaving at any moment. I realised pretty soon that I'd have to leave this compartment, too. When I finally arrived in the next carriage, the best places had already gone, of course. There were only two seats left with Danni and Natascha. Anke was standing pretty helplessly in the corridor.

"Out of order," I **bitched**. "Why didn't you save us a place?"

---

compartment – Abteil;
to fling open – mit Schwung aufmachen;
to growl – knurren; to shove – schieben;
to bitch – meckern

"I saw you getting on further up and thought it was so brilliant I could take my time, Carlotta had everything under control." Anke shook her head. "A bit of a **cock-up**."

"But we can't spend the night standing around out here," I said. "I'll be dead tired in three hours at the most."

"I want to sleep, too," admitted Anke. "The sleep you get before midnight is **particularly** important for the skin. Do you think we could sit next to Natascha after all?"

"No way," I said. "I just don't like her."

"All right," said Anke, "we're friends. We stick together. Neither of us goes to Natascha. But we could ask around if anyone would **swap** with us."

But it was **pointless**. None of the others wanted to give up their seats for us and move into Danni and Natascha's compartment.

"If Danni finds us out here in the corridor, he'll **throw a fit**," said Anke in the end.

"I think he's just **about to**," I said and pulled her into the next compartment. "He's on his way to **count his flock**. Just a second, there's a **spare** seat here."

Tina looked up grudgingly. "So? Stop yelling."

We folded back the armrest and **squeezed** ourselves onto the remaining seat.

---

cock-up – Schlamassel; particularly – besonders;
to swap – tauschen; pointless – zwecklos;
to throw a fit – einen Anfall bekommen;
to be about to do sth. – im Begriff sein etw. zu tun;
to count one's flock – seine Schäfchen zählen;
spare – frei; to squeeze – quetschen

Vera unplugged her Walkman from her ear. "Andrea's in the dining car. She'll be back in about half an hour, but you can sit here till then if you like."

"Thanks so much for your **generous** offer." I said, but Vera was listening to her music again and just smiled politely.

"Just half an hour to sit down, and in this heat," sighed Anke. "When I'm a successful model I'll only take taxis or fly." She tried to open the window, without success.

"You can't turn off the heating," Tina informed us. She took off her shoes and put her feet up. We pulled a face, but did the same after a while. It was incredibly hot and uncomfortable on this train.

"I don't know how we'll survive the night," I murmured while making a kind of pillow out of my pullover and jacket. "If only there was a bit more room."

We played cards for a while, but none of us really enjoyed it. Vera took out her Walkman again and plugged her ears with it. Helena did a crossword puzzle and Tina, who had hardly said a word up to now, reached for her book and held it up in such a way that I could clearly read the title: Literary Miniatures. Typical! She only wanted to make an impression.

"By the way," she said suddenly, "I think you should be going. Andrea will be back soon."

"Let me worry about that!" said Anke nastily. But Tina said she was just telling us.

---

generous – großzügig

I stood up. "There must be two spare seats for us somewhere on this train. I'll go and look. I'll be back in a quarter of an hour at the most."

"You don't need to look very far. Of course there are two spare seats," said Tina with a smile, "in the teachers' compartment."

My **endeavours** seemed to be **in vain**. It was as if half of Germany was on the move that evening. At the dining car I wanted to turn back, when an **elderly** couple with two large suitcases came towards me. Quick as a **flash** I realised that two seats must now be free in the direction they had come from. Just to make sure, I asked the man. He nodded and was about to say something, but I was already running back. I had to take this opportunity before someone else did.

Breathlessly I tore open the compartment door.

Anke looked at me **expectantly**. "Well? Have you found anything?"

I nodded and pulled her into the corridor. "Two seats have just become free behind the dining car. If we hurry ..."

Anke wanted to fetch her shoes, but I stopped her. "It's unbelievably hot all along the train. I haven't got my shoes on either. Come on, hurry up."

We ran the length of the train. It was very difficult to open the door to the carriage beyond the dining car, but we managed it in the end.

---

endeavour – Bemühung; in vain – vergeblich;
elderly – bejahrt; flash – Blitz;
expectant – erwartungsvoll

"Perhaps you're not allowed in here," said Anke. "Can you read what's on that notice?" She pointed to a **mangled** bit of paper someone had **taped** to the door.

I shook my head. "Just hieroglyphics," I reassured her. "But take a look at this."

"Hey, Carlotta, there's no one here," laughed Anke. "We can really stretch out." She yawned loudly. "The others are stupid to sit further up. I wonder why there's no one here?"

"No idea. People probably think the train ends at the dining car. Or they **get put off** because it's so difficult to open the door. What do I know? It doesn't matter anyway. We can lie down for the next six hours, and when we have to change trains we'll have had a good sleep and can make sure we get the best seats."

We drew the curtains, switched off the light and stretched out.

Anke was already yawning. "I'm sure Natascha dyes her hair," she said after a while. "I can see that straight away."

"Of course she does," I said. I could feel myself getting more and more tired.

"I once read about a woman with dyed hair who dived into a swimming pool, and when she came out it was green," Anke told me. "At least that was what it said in the paper recently. It must have been some kind of chemical reaction, but don't ask me what."

"Are you sure she had green hair when she

---

mangled – zerfetzt; to tape – kleben;
to get put off – sich abschrecken lassen

came out of the pool?" I sat up. "Do you think we should suggest going swimming in Erdmanns-weiler?"

We both giggled.

"Imagine Natascha with green hair. Do you think your father would be so **keen on** her then? We should ask Danni about it. Doesn't he teach Chemistry, too?"

I giggled. The warmth and the regular rattling of the train were making me incredibly sleepy. "Wake me up when we have to get off?"

"I've already set the alarm on my watch," whispered Anke. "Good night."

I'm going to be as unfriendly as possible to Natascha, I decided as I fell asleep. It wouldn't be difficult at all. I'd make her realise how it was when someone **snatches** the father away from a divorce **orphan**. 'Divorce orphan' – I'd read the term in some **glossy** recently and thought it fitted me exactly. I was dependent on Dad. And if I got a new mother I wanted to have my say. No Natascha! No way Natascha! "What?" Anke sat up **with a start**. "What's with Natascha?"

"Nothing," I murmured and turned over.

Someone had taken away my **blanket**. Still **drowsy**, I sat up and looked around. Then I finally realised that I wasn't at home in my bed,

---

to be keen on – interessiert sein an;
to snatch – schnappen; orphan – Waise;
glossy – Hochglanzmagazin;
with a start – mit einem Ruck; blanket – Decke;
drowsy – schläfrig

but in a train compartment which had become rather cold. Anke was lying opposite me, snoring quietly. I stood up and investigated **cautiously**. It was almost dark in the compartment. I drew back the curtains. The windows were **steamed up**, and I wiped over them with my hand. Something wasn't right, and suddenly I knew what it was: the train had stopped clattering. We were standing still. 5:23, said my watch. I wasn't at all tired any more and decided to see how the rest of the class was. Perhaps I can take a photo of Natascha sleeping with her mouth open looking stupid, I thought. That would be a nice birthday present for Dad. I giggled softly and Anke sat up.

"Are we there already?" she murmured drowsily. "Do we have to change trains?"

"No, the train's just stopping here," I reassured her. "We're in ..." I pressed my face to the **windowpane**, but I couldn't see any sign. "Well, it doesn't matter. I'll ask Dannitzki where we are."

I looked for my shoes until I remembered I had taken them off yesterday evening in the other compartment and left them there.

Meanwhile Anke had woken up properly. "Are you going up front?" she asked.

I nodded.

"Bring my pullover with you, I'm freezing," she said.

It's quite a long stop, I thought. It was five thirty-three when I tried to pull open the door to the next carriage, but it didn't move one millimetre.

---

cautious – vorsichtig; steamed up – beschlagen; windowpane – Fensterscheibe

I remembered Jenny's **flat refusal** to go anywhere **by rail**. She would rather spend a **fortune** on taxis – better on the nerves, she claimed. And at that moment I could understand what she meant.

"I'm going mad," I murmured, and it was true. I had every reason to. I stared **in dismay** out of the window in the door. "I don't believe it."

"What don't you believe?" asked Anke.

I didn't say a word.

"Hey, what's wrong with you?" Anke had got up and was hopping towards me on one leg. When she saw my shocked expression, she laughed. "It's against cellulite – **flabby** legs, you know. I do exercises for them every morning. You have to start these things in good time and ..."

"I'm afraid your flabby legs are the least of our worries," I said. "Take a look outside."

"We've been **uncoupled**!" she cried. "They've lost us!"

Anke had immediately realised what had **dawned on** me three minutes before. It wasn't the train that had a long stop here, but only our carriage. We were standing in a **siding** and the rest of our class had continued on their way ...

Anke laughed out loud. "Now we know why there was no one in the carriage. We're so **dumb**. Do you think they'll have missed us already?"

---

flat – *hier:* pauschal; refusal – Ablehnung;
by rail – mit dem Zug; fortune – Vermögen;
in dismay – bestürzt; flabby – schwabbelig;
to uncouple – abkoppeln; to dawn on sb. – jmdm. dämmern; siding – Abstellgleis; dumb – doof

Ten minutes

later we were creeping into the station building. Quite **literally** creeping, because we didn't have any shoes on and were freezing cold. Anke cheered up for a moment when she saw an **indicator** announcing a train to Berlin in half an hour.

"That's got to be the **proverbial** call of destiny," she said. "We *had* to get uncoupled here because **fate** has bigger things **in store** for me. What do you think? We'll just go to Berlin and see what happens."

"*You* can go to Berlin and see what happens," I said, marching towards the only open ticket window, behind which sat an overworked railway **employee** who was staring at my tennis socks in disbelief.

Anke ran after me. "What's wrong with you? Come with me. Imagine the trouble Natascha will get into if we go missing," she said. "That's **neglect** of **legal responsibility** and stuff like that."

---

literally – wörtlich; indicator – Anzeigetafel;
proverbial – sprichwörtlich; fate – Schicksal;
to have sth. in store – etw. bereithalten;
employee – Angestellter;
neglect – Vernachlässigung, Missachtung;
legal responsibility – Aufsichtspflicht

I **gulped**. She did have a point. I wasn't exactly keen to go to Berlin, but giving Natascha a good scare was worth a thing or two. I was just about to say yes when I **caught sight of** the man behind the ticket window. He had stood up and was **bending** forward with interest. For a moment I had the feeling he was suppressing a grin at the sight of us two **pathetic** creatures.

"Your socks have seen better days," he said pointing to my feet. "Where have you two come from?"

We sat in the cold of the station for half an hour in front of a model of a **steam** train from 1848, until the ticket **clerk** told us that someone from the youth hostel in Erdmannsweiler was coming to collect us. "I'm supposed to keep you here so you arrive properly this time," he laughed. "Your teacher has also been informed. Oh dear, oh dear, I wouldn't like **to be in your shoes** – or rather, in your socks!"

"What do you think? Will Danni be really annoyed?" asked Anke. She seemed a little worried.

I **hummed and hawed** and said he ought to be happy that we'd turned up again, and anyway, it was the railway's fault because the notice ...

---

to gulp – schlucken;
to catch sight of sb./sth. – jmdn/etw. erblicken;
to bend – sich beugen; pathetic – mitleiderregend;
steam – Dampf; clerk – Schalterbeamte/-r;
to be in someone's shoes – in jmds. Haut stecken;
to hum and haw – herumdrucksen

But Anke wasn't listening to me any more. Her eyes were wide open and she was mumbling, "I'm going crazy!"

I turned in the direction she was looking and saw a man **weighed down** with cameras walking around **inquisitively**.

"You see," whispered Anke, "I told you I was going to be discovered."

I couldn't suppress my laughter. "Have you taken a look in the mirror this morning?" I asked. "You look wrecked."

"That's the new look," she claimed. "Most models have rings under their eyes and look wrecked." But she didn't really seem sure of herself.

The man had come closer and was **aiming** his camera in our direction.

"What did I tell you?" whispered Anke. "You'll be in the photo, too, with any luck."

"Could I ask you two ladies for a favour?" I must have looked unsure of myself, because the man laughed. "Don't worry, I'm from the press."

"Didn't I tell you?" murmured Anke stretching herself a little.

"Why are you here so early?" I enquired.

The man laughed once again. "Good question," he said. "I want to take some pictures in the station for a railway magazine, and in a couple of hours all hell breaks loose here. I'd like to photograph the steam train behind you. Could you move a little to the side?"

---

weighed down – beladen; inquisitive – neugierig; to aim – zielen, *hier:* richten auf

Luckily, the man who was going to take us to Erdmannsweiler **turned up** at this moment, and the photographer was spared Anke's **curses**.

She was totally frustrated. "Someone give me an **anaesthetic**," she mumbled and **curled up** in her seat. Then she discovered a **tattered** pop magazine and flicked through it with interest. "There's nothing wrong with it, but my mother throws a fit whenever I want to buy one," she said. "Listen to what it says here: 'How to get your dream boy. A thousand tips and tricks for clever girls.' It's interesting, that kind of thing!"

She read out at least ten of the thousand tips and tricks in a loud voice, but I was just too tired to listen. And anyway, my mind went back to Dad and Natascha. Perhaps it was the real thing between them, and I didn't stand a chance. Two years before I had also fallen in love, but it can't have been the love of my life because when he moved away I soon forgot about him. But perhaps it was different between Dad and the new one, and ...

"Are you listening to me?" asked Anke and threw the magazine onto the seat beside her.

The driver grinned and said of course he had **been all ears** the whole time, and he wanted to ask his wife if she had used tricks like that on him. "But perhaps there's something in there about cars. I'm more interested in *them*, to be

---

to turn up – auftauchen; curse – Fluch;
anaesthetic – Narkose;
to curl up – es sich gemütlich machen;
tattered – zerfleddert; to be all ears – ganz Ohr sein

honest," he added. "Fast cars, if you want to know. My sister has an Italian sports car, and what does she do with it? Uses it to go shopping and have coffee on Sundays! And of course she never lets me drive it." He **frowned**. "I have to drive this old **crate** instead. But we'll soon be in Erdmannsweiler, and if I'm not very much mistaken we're expected."

How right he was. The whole class, Mr Dannitzki and Natascha were standing in front of the youth hostel and they laughed as we got out of the car.

"Our lost daughters return. I should really give you two an **almighty telling-off**," said Mr Dannitzki, but you could hear the relief in his voice that we had turned up **unharmed**. "If I have even the slightest trouble with you, I'll send you back home immediately **at** your parents' **expense**. Have I made myself clear? You don't think I'm going to go grey **on your account**!"

"Danni should be grateful he still *has* some hair, even if it does go grey," Anke whispered to me. "We promise never to leave your side, Mr Dannitzki," she said out loud.

Danni looked horrified and fled into the youth hostel. I was about to carry my things inside when I saw Natascha. She took a step towards me. For the briefest moment I thought she was

---

to frown – die Stirn runzeln; crate – Kiste;
almighty – mordsmäßig; telling-off – Standpauke;
unharmed – unverletzt;
at sb's expense – auf jmds. Kosten;
on your account – *hier:* euretwegen

going to take me in her arms. But then she stood still and just said, "I've been so worried about you."

I'd most like to have said, "So? If I hadn't turned up again, you'd have had Dad all to yourself in no time." But I was too tired to argue, and anyway, half the class was standing there and I didn't want to put on a show for them. I just **shrugged my shoulders** and turned my back.

The **titchiest** room in the hostel was left over for Anke and me, with a **wobbly bunk bed** and an extra camp bed. The lower bunk was already taken.

"And who's sleeping here? Who does this rabbit belong to?" asked Anke pointing to a **soft toy** that was lying on the bed. "If we have Tina in our room, I'm going to Berlin and that's a promise."

"Me, too, Anke, believe me," I assured her, and really meant it this time.

But we were in luck again. Stefanie came into the room. She stuffed the rabbit under the bedcovers in embarrassment. "Danni's going to give a **slide show** about the area here," she told us, "and if we aren't all downstairs in three minutes he'll be furious."

"A slide show," groaned Anke. "Slide shows are the worst."

We were looking at probably the three-hundred-

---

to shrug one's shoulders – mit den Schultern zucken;
titchy – winzig; wobbly – wackelig;
bunk bed – Stockbett; soft toy – Kuscheltier;
slide show – Diashow

and-sixty-second slide when the bell went for lunch.

"**Stew**," announced Andrea, rolling her eyes. "Just imagine, there's stew. I read it just now on the notice board."

Mr Dannitzki gave her a reproachful look. "What's wrong with stew? There's a real art to a good stew. My wife always says a stew needs ..."

I knew I had to find a seat a long way from our Maths teacher for lunch.

And far away from Natascha, who was already sitting down and smiling at me. "It tastes lovely," she claimed and **dipped** her spoon into the **gooey** mess.

I ignored her and squeezed in next to Tina, who looked up **stroppily**. "Can't you see there's no room here?"

Silly cow, I thought and beamed at her. "No, I can't." I laid my arms on the table possessively. Heike, who was sitting opposite me, grinned. She couldn't stand Tina either.

"**Discretion is the better part of valour**," said Tina, who carefully placed her spoon and paper **napkin** into her bowl and stood up.

I was about to make a **derisive** remark about her – along the lines of "Now she'll go and comfort herself with Goethe" – when Mr Dannitzki made his way up to our table.

---

stew – Eintopf; to dip – eintauchen;
gooey – zähflüssig; stroppy – patzig;
Discretion is the better part of valour. – Vorsicht ist besser als Nachsicht.; napkin – Serviette;
derisive – hämisch

"We saved a place for you," **fawned** Andrea. And she certainly needed to suck up to the Maths teacher.

"Well, how do you like Erdmannsweiler?" he asked good-humouredly. "Have I **sung** its **praises** too highly?"

Some of the girls said how great it was here, what with the landscape and the youth hostel and everything. Our Maths teacher gave a satisfied **nod**. "We start exploring the area at three this afternoon. Did I ever tell you that I originally wanted to study Geography? No? Well, some of the old enthusiasm is still there, and I hope I'll be able to tell you a thing or two later."

I couldn't wait. He'd probably examine every single stone and tell us what millennium it came from. I knew this from Dad. If he sees a museum on the horizon, he **rattles off** his entire scientific knowledge. If I ever have children, I'll definitely do things differently.

"So, ladies, front door, half past two **sharp**. With **sturdy** shoes, rain jackets and perhaps a bag for **rock samples**."

"Do you really want to go in sandals?" I asked Anke in disbelief. "I mean, Danni wants to hike until at least half past six. At least that's what he said at lunch."

"That's exactly why I'm putting my sandals

---

to fawn – schleimen; to sing praises – loben;
nod – Nicken; to rattle off – *hier:* herunterrasseln;
sharp – *hier:* Punkt, pünktlich; sturdy – fest, stabil;
rock sample – Gesteinsprobe

on," she laughed. "You don't think I'm going to march through the middle of nowhere for that long. Anyway, I haven't got any other shoes with me."

Of course Mr Dannitzki saw Anke was wearing the wrong shoes straight away, and got all worked up about it. Then he told her to change into some proper shoes and to get a move on, it was already twenty-five to three and he'd planned an **extensive** programme and did he always have to make an exception for her?

"But I've just said I haven't got any walking boots or any other sturdy shoes with me," explained Anke, and for a moment it looked as if our Maths teacher was going to have a heart attack.

"All right," he said finally, "then borrow a pair from one of your classmates."

Anke grinned. "Fine. Does anyone take size 42?"

Of course no one put their hand up. Anke was lying, because recently I had borrowed her trainers in Sports and they fitted me okay. Her feet couldn't possibly have grown two sizes in three weeks.

Mr Dannitzki looked quickly down at his own shoes – he probably took size 42 – but then he shook his head. "Then you'll have to go like that. But it won't be any fun, I can assure you. We'll be hiking up hill and down **dale**."

And we did hike up hill and down dale. Roads

---

extensive – umfangreich; dale – Tal

seemed completely unnecessary to our Maths teacher. "We're not on a Sunday **stroll**," he said when Andrea refused to crawl under some **barbed wire**, "so don't **make** such **a fuss**."

At around half past three there was a **moderate** shower which transformed the fields into a **swamp**. "I think we'll have to send you home," said Natascha with a look at Anke's sandals. "It's a pity because Mr Dannitzki's going to show us something very special in a moment or two, but ..." She **gestured vaguely** and probably felt she was being particularly educational.

But Anke had been waiting for this. Yes, she was terribly sorry she couldn't go on with us, she said, and she would see if the youth hostel had some shoes in her size.

"Can we let you go back alone?" wondered Mr Dannitzki out loud. "If you lose your way I'll be in deep trouble. No, it's out of the question. Sorry, Anke, my dear, but I'm afraid you'll have to stay on the hike **despite** the weather and your footwear problems," and he gave her a really mean grin.

But Anke was in luck. As we were crossing a country road five minutes later, Natascha gave a shout and waved to a bright yellow sports car, which drove up slowly and came to a halt. "I'll ask if Anke can have a **lift** back to Erd-

---

stroll – Spaziergang; barbed wire – Stacheldrahtzaun; to make a fuss – sich anstellen; moderate – *hier:* leicht; swamp – Sumpf, Morast; to gesture – gestikulieren; vague – unbestimmt, vage; despite – trotz; lift – Mitfahrgelegenheit

mannsweiler," she explained to Danni, who seemed quite **baffled**. "It's the warden of the youth hostel. Don't you recognise the car?"

Danni apologised for his **abominable** memory, said he'd be glad to be able to **distinguish** a **tri-cycle** from a Mercedes and told Anke to make herself useful at the youth hostel.

"Hey," I whispered to her, "you were lucky with those sandals."

Anke shrugged her shoulders. "Well, an after-noon in the youth hostel isn't much fun either. I'll lie down for a little and then find out if they have a video at least."

She waved goodbye, Danni clapped his hands and we had to continue our hike, **urged on** by our teacher's promise to show us something special.

"What do you think it could be?" asked Heike and joined arms with Stefanie, who was walking next to me.

I shook my head. "No idea. I only know that when teachers want to show you something, it's usually educational. Perhaps he wants to show us a **cowslip**."

Heike laughed. "You're probably right. But what do you think about the warden's car? You'd never think she drove an Italian sports car."

At some point we realised we were going round in circles, and that Mr Dannitzki hadn't found what he'd been looking for all this time.

---

baffled – perplex; abominable – furchtbar schlecht; to distinguish – unterscheiden; tricycle – Dreirad; to urge sb. on – jmdn. anspornen, antreiben; cowslip – Schlüsselblume

"Supper's at half past six. We ought to get back," remarked Natascha quietly.

It was the first **sensible** thing she had said.

Mr Dannitzki nodded. "But we won't give up so soon," he said. "We'll take up the search tomorrow. I found it last year after all."

"I'm afraid Anke was right," I said.

"What do you mean?" Stefanie carefully made her way alongside a muddy **puddle** and then turned round to me.

"I mean with Berlin. We'll be bored to death here. There's nothing here except rocks and weird flowers."

"Actually, I love it when there's nothing to do for a change," she said. And then she told us about her home life until we got back to the youth hostel.

Anke ran out of the building straight away. She was still wearing her sandals, but seemed to be in a really good mood. No wonder, I thought, she's been asleep the whole afternoon and now she feels fine.

"Well, I hope you amused yourselves," she laughed as she saw our exhausted faces.

I wanted to say something, but the right words didn't come to me quickly enough.

"By the way, I've tidied up our room and got in some **supplies**," she said **soothingly**, "because there's a bit of a problem with the evening meal. Something went wrong with our booking and we're not on the list for tonight."

---

sensible – vernünftig; puddle – Pfütze;
supplies – Vorräte; soothing – besänftigend

"Does that mean we're not getting anything to eat?" Tina cried out indignantly. Anke beamed at her. "Exactly, my dear Tina. But people like you who are always giving themselves food for thought don't need to eat very much, do they?"

"But we ate at lunchtime," said Mr Dannitzki in surprise. And anyway, I told them, 150 percent, that we wanted lunch *and* supper today."

"We only got lunch today because the other class staying here went on an **outing** from seven until quarter past three, while we **scoffed their nosh**. And apart from that I don't think you can have more than a hundred percent," added Anke.

"Higher mathematics, but you don't get it until next year," grinned Mr Dannitzki. "Right, this evening there'll be no activities and you'll all make sure you go to bed early. I think we're still stressed out from the journey. At five o'clock tomorrow morning we'll meet in the **meadow** behind the hostel to listen to the birdsong. I've brought a bird-call **whistle** with me, and you'll be amazed how many **species** answer."

"And what about the evening meal?" somebody called.

"Experiments with rats have shown that a lower food intake **increases life expectancy**. I'll explain it to you in more detail next year, when you've got me for Biology."

---

outing – Ausflug;
to scoff someone's nosh – jmds. Essen wegmampfen;
meadow – Wiese; whistle – Pfeife; species – Art;
to increase – erhöhen; life expectancy – Lebenserwartung

"But I'm not a rat. And my mother's always saying I'm too thin," said Vera. "Think of the fuss she'd make if I came home even thinner."

Danni certainly didn't want to get into trouble with Vera's mother. "I'll ask in the kitchen if we can have some bread, sausage and cheese," he **relented**. "You can make sandwiches in your rooms if we can't use the dining room this evening."

Some of the class began to **grumble**. The hike had been ridiculous, and now we had to make our own supper. "Don't work yourselves up," said Anke. "Just be glad there isn't stew again like at lunchtime."

Our room might have been the smallest of all, but Anke had made it cosy. There were blue serviettes laid out on the little table, in the middle stood a candle – only the matches were missing – and next to it lay bags of pretzels and crisps.

"And here," she said pointing under the table, "are six bottles of lemonade. That should do for a start, I think. And for dessert there's chocolate. You don't need to give me any money, by the way. It's my **treat**."

"Is it your birthday or something, Anke?" inquired Stefanie **suspiciously**.

Anke shook her head. "No. But I've got to like Erdmannsweiler quite a lot. A really **cute** little village."

"Erdmannsweiler?" I'd got used to Anke be-

---

to relent – nachgeben; to grumble – motzen;
treat – besonderes Vergnügen; suspicious – misstrauisch;
cute – nett

ing a bit **quirky**, but her suddenly finding the village cute seemed really weird to me.

Anke had stuffed a handful of crisps into her mouth and was giving me a hard stare. Suddenly she had a coughing fit. Tears ran down her cheeks, and for a moment I had the feeling that this was more than just something going down the wrong way.

"You're my **mates**," she said looking at us **conspiratorially**, "so what I'm about to tell you stays in this room, do you understand?"

Stefanie and I nodded.

"Say loudly and clearly that you swear not to say a word to ..."

"**Lay off the suspense**," I said, **stifling** a yawn.

Stefanie nodded. "We walked at least ten kilometres while you were having a rest. Do you think I'll be able to get a **hot-water bottle** around here? My feet are freezing, and that's the first sign of a cold. That's what my mother always says."

"Do you swear?"

"Yes, we swear!" Stefanie and I assured her.

With an air of importance Anke poured lemonade into the toothbrush glasses. "Just imagine, I ..." She paused for a moment and **stirred** her lemonade with her middle finger. "I've fallen in love. I'm so happy I could cry." Her eyes shone strangely.

---

quirky – schrullig; mate – Freund, Kumpel;
conspiratorial – verschwörerisch;
Lay off the suspense. – Spann uns nicht länger auf die Folter.; to stifle – unterdrücken;
hot-water bottle – Wärmflasche, to stir – umrühren

"Very nice," said Stefanie, unmoved. "Have you got anything against me going to look for a hot-water bottle?"

"Sometimes I think Stefanie's absolutely impossible. Cold, you could almost say," Anke complained to me once Stefanie had left the room. "I mean, I tell you both I'm in love, and all she thinks about is her hot-water bottle. But at least you understand me, don't you, Carlotta?"

"Of course I understand you," I said although I was terribly tired. "Who have you fallen in love with?"

Anke laughed dreamily. "He looks so sweet." She closed her eyes. "He's got dark blond hair, not too short. His eyes are ..." She shook her head. "I couldn't see them, it all went so quickly. It was as if I'd been **struck by lightning**. At any rate, he looks really sweet." She looked at me. "What do you think?"

I thought for a moment. "What's his name? Where does he live? Here in the youth hostel or where?"

Anke laughed. "I don't know his name yet. I saw him in the village at the baker's. He probably lives in Erdmannsweiler. At least I suppose so. Hey, Carlotta, I'm so happy."

"Great," I said, thinking I sounded pretty half-hearted. "And what are you going to do now?"

"I want to see him again, of course, that's obvious. But how am I going to find him? I've made some **enquiries**: Erdmannsweiler has ex-

---

to be struck by lightning – vom Blitz getroffen sein;
to make enquiries – Nachforschungen anstellen

actly 5789 inhabitants." She looked at me helplessly.

Jenny says that Dad has a thing about helping people. He's always offering to help everyone, and that's probably how he got to know Natascha and all his other girlfriends. And the fact is, I've **inherited** this from him. I couldn't do anything else except say, "Anke, I'll help you. For sure."

"**Amazing**," she said happily, "I knew you'd say that. At least I can count on you."

"We don't need to call on everyone in Erdmannsweiler," I thought out loud. "How old is your **guy**, **approximately**?"

"Perhaps one or two years older than me, at a guess," said Anke. "I **got such a crush on** him I couldn't concentrate on things like that."

"Of course," I said, and for a moment wished I could fall in love, too. "So this means he must still go to school. Let's take a walk past the school, just **on the off-chance**, and have a look."

Anke threw her arms around my neck. "Great idea. I'll grant you every wish."

"Fine," I said. "I'll tell you the first one straight away. I help you get to know the boy, and you help me **annoy** Natascha."

---

to inherit – erben; amazing – *hier:* toll;
guy – Bursche, Kerl; approximately – ungefähr;
to get a crush on sb. – sich in jmdn. verknallen;
on the off-chance – auf gut Glück;
to annoy – ärgern, nerven

Before going to sleep

Anke had murmured something about setting the alarm for half past six. We really needed to discuss a few things, but it was already quarter past nine when someone banged on our door and shouted, "Get up **sleepyheads**, or you'll miss breakfast!"

"What's all this shouting?" muttered Anke as she **fiddled about** with the buttons on her alarm clock. "I don't know why this stupid thing doesn't work." She looked at me questioningly. "Or did you turn the alarm off?"

I shook my head. "We should get a move on, otherwise we really will miss breakfast. Just remember yesterday's supper."

We were the last to appear in the dining room. All the other tables had already been cleared. Mr Dannitzki was standing at the window looking **gloomily** out at the rain. "Didn't you eat everything up yesterday, or why is the weather so bad?" he asked us. "And may I ask you to get up a little earlier in future? This isn't a hotel after all."

"Perhaps we overslept because of the change of air," I said and pointed vaguely in the direc-

---

sleepyhead – Schlafmütze;
to fiddle about – herumfummeln; gloomy – bedrückt

tion of the pile of maps on one of the tables. "Are we going hiking again today?"

"Of course we are!" Mr Dannitzki grinned. "The weather can only get better, and you ought to see something of the area. By the way, you **stood me up** this morning."

Damn, the birdsong! "Sorry, Mr Dannitzki, but ..." I stuttered, but Danni just laughed.

"I understand. I was the same when I was young. But we're definitely going hiking today."

"In this rotten weather?" Anke almost **choked** on her food. "Couldn't we just stay here? I don't mean in the youth hostel, but ... Well, we could take a closer look at Erdmannsweiler. It's supposed to be such a nice little village, and it would be a pity not to have seen it."

Our Maths teacher looked at us **disconcertedly**. "You want to take a look at Erdmannsweiler? I'm astonished, Anke, my dear. Weren't you complaining about going to a **one-horse town** instead of Berlin? Have you completely changed your mind?"

Anke laughed **awkwardly**. "Sorry, but I really have changed my mind. I think we should give Erdmannsweiler a chance. You said yourself that these Saxon villages have a charm of their own and ..."

"Well then, go and look at the village," laughed Danni and folded up his maps. "At some point it'll stop raining, and then we'll go hiking, okay?"

---

to stand sb. up – jmdn. versetzen;
to choke – ersticken; disconcerted – verdutzt;
one-horse town – Kaff; awkward – unbeholfen

Anke beamed. "Come on, Carlotta, let's go to the village."

At first I wanted to say no – I really didn't fancy walking around outside in this weather. But then I remembered why Anke wanted to go there. I was about to suggest at least waiting until it had stopped raining, when I saw Natascha coming towards us. She waved and wanted to say something. I turned away. "Come on, Anke, let's go."

"Perhaps I should buy a pair of **weatherproof** hiking boots," **mused** Anke after the two kilometres to the village.

She hadn't said a word the whole time, which for Anke is completely abnormal. Instead she seemed to have been thinking about things and to have come to some sort of conclusion. She put her arm in mine and laughed. "It's raining, and my sandals are full of water, but I'm the happiest person alive. And it's so good of you to come with me. But where on earth are we going?"

"Well, I thought we'd go to the school and check out the situation."

Anke laughed. "Sure, I'd completely forgotten. It'll soon be time for the break."

We asked a woman who was cleaning her windows where the school was and marched on through the **drizzle**. Before we got there, we could already see that the break had started.

"We'll just stand at the edge of the schoolyard

---

weatherproof – wetterfest;
to muse – grübeln;
drizzle – Nieselregen

and watch," I suggested. "If you see him, give me a sign."

"And then?" Anke looked at me questioningly. "What will we do then?"

I hadn't got a clue, but I wasn't going to admit *that* in a hurry. "I'll think of something," I told her.

The schoolyard was full of people, but I soon saw that we were in the wrong place. "Primary school, Anke. I hardly think yesterday's guy was an eight-year-old, or am I wrong?"

"But why is there just a primary school here? I mean, children get older, too, and . . ."

"... then they go to the **county town**," said a man next to us. "That's the way it goes."

Anke looked totally frustrated. To cheer her up, I bought three pieces of **custard cake** in the bakery and offered her one of them on the way back. But she wasn't hungry and she was in a bad mood.

"You know what, my mother always says, 'Have **confidence** in yourself. **Speak your mind**. Don't be shy in front of your dream boy.' She says I should act **liberated**."

"The only thing is, you have to find him again." It just came out, and immediately I was sorry I'd said it.

Anke pulled a handful of leaves from the **hedge** by the road and threw them into the air. She was almost crying.

---

county town – Kreisstadt; custard cake – Cremetorte;
confidence – Vertrauen;
to speak one's mind – seine Meinung sagen;
liberated – emanzipiert; hedge – Hecke

"Perhaps you should have asked the woman in the bakery about him. Why didn't you do that?"

"Because everything always goes wrong. Because everything's stupid. Another woman was there yesterday. But I'll go back this afternoon, even if I have to stand around in the shop for an hour. Perhaps he'll turn up again. You just can't imagine how I feel."

She seemed quite worked up. I wanted to say something nice to her, but I knew it was **pointless**. Anke *wanted* to **work herself up** at the moment. She'd get back to normal pretty soon. Actually, I had more reason to get worked up than she did. After all, I'd walked through the rain on her account. I was about to say so when she turned to me in front of the youth hostel. "And while we're feeling annoyed, I'm going to reception to complain about our tiny room. It's outrageous."

"But Anke," I said, "we arrived too late and ..."

She gave a brief laugh. "No, I simply don't see why we should have such a titchy room. And the wallpaper! Have you taken a closer look at it?" She **was raring to** go and there was no stopping her. "And you're coming with me," she said, **dragging** me behind her. She was probably behaving the way her mother always expected her to and she strode up to the reception desk.

There was a lot going on in the entrance hall.

---

pointless – zwecklos; to work onself up – sich aufregen; to be raring to do sth. – *hier:* entschlossen sein zu etw.; to drag – ziehen

A class – probably the one that had been on an outing the day before – had just come back from a hike. Their teacher was wiping the condensation off his glasses and shouting "Quiet!" every now and then. But he could have saved his breath because no one was listening to him. I'd have preferred to just slip away, but I didn't want Anke to think I was a **coward** so I went to her side.

"And what do *you* want?" said the woman at the reception desk. She looked pretty annoyed and turned to the teacher. "Mr Jessing, could you please make them calm down?"

The man raised his hands **in appeasement**. "You can go and watch a video," he shouted into the **din**. For a moment it really was quiet, but only for a moment. Then the argument started about which video to watch.

"So, now you. What can I do for you?" asked the woman, trying to smile.

"I want to complain," said Anke. "About our room. I think our **accommodation** is a **disgrace**. My friend here thinks so, too." She turned to me. I wanted the ground to swallow me up I was so embarrassed.

But if I had expected Anke to push me to the front, I was mistaken. She was looking in my direction all right, but suddenly she seemed very unsure of herself.

---

coward – Feigling;
in appeasement – besänftigend;
din – Radau; accommodation – Unterbringung;
disgrace – Schande

"Complain?" asked the woman. "Do you think ..."

Anke had gone red all over. "No, everything's fine," she stuttered. "It was just a joke."

Without looking at me she ran upstairs, probably to our room.

"And you? Do you want to complain as well?"

I shook my head. "No, not at all." Then I ran after Anke.

"What was *that* all about? First you make an enormous fuss and then ..."

"Carlotta, **miracles** really *do* happen. I knew today was my lucky day." Anke was dancing up and down and round and round. "You've no idea, you've no idea," she sang and wrapped her arms around me.

"But you'll tell me, I suppose."

"Do you know who was standing behind you just now? The boy from the bakery! That's fate, isn't it? Hey, did I talk a lot of rubbish? Do you think he heard all that about wanting to complain and stuff? And what should I do now?" Anke started biting one of her light-blue-**varnished** nails.

"Just go up to him and say you think he's nice and you'd like to get to know him," I suggested.

Anke shook her head **vigorously**. "I can't right now. I don't know why. In theory it wouldn't be a problem, but I just can't at the moment." She looked angrily at her fingernails. "And today of all days I haven't got any blue nail varnish with

---

miracle – Wunder; varnished – lackiert;
vigorous – energisch

me. Say something, Carlotta. You always have such good ideas." She looked at me as if she was going to cry.

"But that's great," I said. "At least we know now that he's here in the youth hostel. So we're more than likely to run into him again, don't you think?"

Anke swallowed. "You're probably right. And what will I do then?"

"Ask him the time, perhaps?"

Anke pulled a face. "I don't think relationships start like that. In films, perhaps, but in reality? He'll just say half past two and walk away."

The door to our room opened and Stefanie came in. "What are you doing here?" she asked in astonishment.

I muttered a few words, but Stefanie wasn't particularly interested. She was **ecstatic**. "Just imagine, behind the building there's a field of horses and two lovely **foals**, and we can even go riding. And tonight we're **putting on** a play."

"Great," said Anke, without much enthusiasm. "I thought we were going to watch a video."

Stefanie giggled. "Stupid Tina has managed to break the video player. No wonder, considering the film she tried to **insert** this morning. Something about the minnesong of Walther von der Vogelweide, or whatever his name is. And the machine went on strike, of course. So tonight

---

ecstatic – ekstatisch; foal – Fohlen;
to put on – *hier:* inszenieren;
to insert – *hier:* einlegen

we're putting on a play. Natascha's getting everything ready."

"Oh yeah?" I said. "Has Natascha taken over now and is telling us what to do?"

"I think Natasha's great." Stefanie gave me a friendly look. "It's a real piece of luck she's with us, don't you think?"

I **forced** myself to smile, but inside I was raging. Who was Dad's new girlfriend trying to **kid**? If she thought she could use her acting skills to win over half the class, and in the end me too, she was much mistaken. I looked at Anke, who frowned. "Does it have to be this evening?" She didn't feel like doing a play with Natascha either, but for different reasons.

Stefanie nodded. "It'll be a wonderful experience to see a real actress at work. By the way, we're going to look at an old **mill** in ten minutes. Hurry up, you two."

During the walk to the mill I had a good think. There had to be some way of **upsetting** Natascha's balance this evening. But no matter how much I **brooded over** the problem I couldn't come up with anything. I couldn't expect any help from Anke. All she was thinking about was how she'd seen the boy again.

"Don't worry," she whispered. "We'll get through this evening. We don't need to clap. If you want, I can whistle and boo."

---

to force – zwingen; to kid – *hier:* täuschen;
mill – Mühle; to upset – *hier:* erschüttern;
to brood over – brüten über

A little after eight we all met up in the dining room, where Natascha was already waiting. She was wearing black leggings and a black roll-neck sweater, and I thought she looked really weird. She frowned at the cassette player in front of her, asked Heike to operate it for her, and then turned to us.

"First I'm going to read you a short summary of the play – it's one of Shakespeare's less well-known ones, by the way, and we modernised it, as you'll see and hear. Then I'll act a few scenes, or at least **extracts** from them. It would be great if some of you would be **brave** enough to take part. I'll tell you exactly what to do."

Dreary, I thought, how boring, and I remembered the first time Dad had taken me to the theatre. I had really only put 'theatre' on my Christmas list **for his sake**, and I imagined a kind of fairytale with a beautiful princess and a brave prince and perhaps a **wicked** witch who'd be **defeated** in the end. But no way! Dad chose a modern play that he probably didn't understand himself but had got excellent **reviews**, as he told me later in **justification**. Men in everyday clothes stood around on the stage and screamed their lines at the audience. At some point Dad had to leave because some people complained about the crying child next to him. That was his first and last **attempt** to get me interested in the theatre.

---

extract – Auszug; brave – mutig; dreary – langweilig; for sb.'s sake – jmdm. zuliebe; wicked – *hier:* böse; to defeat – besiegen; review – *hier:* Kritik; justification – Rechtfertigung; attempt – Versuch

At first I was afraid Natascha would get me up to the front. I decided I'd just refuse. She could hardly force me. But the more I thought about it, the better I liked the idea of taking part. I could act stupid and make her say the wrong thing and **show her true colours**. She'd probably **yell** and scream, and then I could say quite coolly, "I'm sure Dad won't like you shouting at me." There were enough witnesses. Danni would probably **intervene** if Natascha behaved badly.

I took a discreet look around. Mr Dannitzki was leaning on one of the tables that had been pushed into a corner and kept nodding his head **in approval**. Hadn't he once **confessed** to us during a school outing that he was a scientist through and through and didn't have a clue about literature? He was probably only pretending to be enthusiastic so as not to make a **fool** of himself in front of Natascha.

Tina was holding a yellow Reclam booklet in front of her face and seemed to be concentrating on following the text, although there wasn't a German teacher she could **impress** for miles around.

"I need someone to bring me a message. I'm Elizabeth the First, and ceremony is very strict at my **court**." Natascha leaned forward and inspected us.

---

to show one's true colours – sein wahres Gesicht zeigen;
to yell – schreien; to intervene – eingreifen;
in approval – zustimmend; to confess – zugeben;
fool – Dummkopf; to impress – beeindrucken;
court – Hof

Most of the class looked shyly at the floor. This was my chance. I raised my hand.

Anke looked at me in astonishment. "I thought you wanted to boycott her," she whispered.

I didn't have time to explain my plan to Anke. "I'd like to take part," I said loudly.

Did I imagine it, or did Natascha really seem a little uncertain? She hesitated a moment. "I'm glad you **volunteered**, Carlotta. But you may not be right for this role. You need to be able to dance the twist."

The twist? I'd heard of it, but I'd no idea what it was. Something to do with sewing? Everyone had turned round to look at me. There was no going back.

"No problem," I claimed and was about to stand up and go to the front when Natascha stopped me with a wave.

"Fine. But I do see a small problem with the second and third **conditions**. You need to be about 120 years old and almost **bald**."

I was sure she'd just made this up, but the class **howled with glee**. Anke was laughing out loud as well.

Natascha beamed. "Mr Dannitzki," she called, "for the next scene I need you."

Danni could hardly breathe, he was laughing so much. "120 and almost bald! Is that how you see me? I have to warn you – I'm completely untalented."

---

to volunteer – sich freiwillig melden;
condition – Bedingung; bald – kahl;
to howl with glee – brüllen vor Lachen

Natascha shook her head. "No one is completely untalented," she said. "I'm sure you can dance the twist."

"When I was young, yes," admitted our Maths teacher. "The last time I danced the twist was 40 years ago."

Natascha gave Heike a sign, 1950s music rang out and Danni actually stood up and danced. People were almost falling off their chairs, they were laughing so much. Only I was not amused. Perhaps I should call Dad and tell him about Natascha's behaviour. But he probably wouldn't understand.

After three minutes Danni stopped, gasping for breath. "Enough, enough," he cried, "I'm an old man after all."

"**Encore**, encore," some people called, but Danni waved them aside.

"If I go on like that, we won't be able to go hiking tomorrow."

"That would be heaven," called out Anke next to me, and a few girls cheered.

"Now's a good opportunity. Let's get out of here," I whispered to Anke, but she didn't look at me. "Are you coming?" I asked a little louder, and immediately people turned round **in annoyance** and hissed, "Quiet!"

"Ssh," said Anke, too. "This Natascha is a **gem**! I'll tell you later."

---

encore – Zugabe; in annoyance – verärgert; gem – Juwel

"What's up with you?" asked Anke when we were together in the washroom. "You have to admit it was funny seeing Danni dancing. Are you annoyed?"

"**Dead right**," I said. "We agreed not to clap. And whose idea was it to boo?"

Anke looked at me **in consternation**. "You're one to talk. First you put your hand up and say you want to take part, and now this. I was surprised, but I assumed you'd thought about it and ..."

"I'd have given Natascha some aggro if she'd let me take part," I assured Anke.

"Too bad," murmured Anke, rubbing her face with **cleansing milk**. "I still don't know what you mean."

"It doesn't matter," I said.

"But Carlotta, honestly – you mustn't be angry with me – I thought it was a wonderful evening. Because ..." She paused **briefly**.

I didn't give her any help. "Because?"

"You know, when she read out that bit with the queen's **servant**, who played **go-between** for her because she couldn't ask her **admirer** if he wanted to marry her, it suddenly became clear to me how we had to do it. Diplomatically. I just need a go-between."

"Good for you," I said, looking for my toothbrush. It had been in my **sponge bag** that morn-

---

dead right – goldrichtig; in consternation – bestürzt; cleansing milk – Reinigungsmilch; brief – kurz; servant – Diener/-in; go-between – Vermittler/-in; admirer – *hier:* Verehrer; sponge bag – Kulturbeutel

ing. I shook the contents into one of the **sinks**. A toothbrush can't just disappear. "And where are you going to get a go-between?"

Anke swallowed. "I was thinking of you."

"Me?"

"Come on, Carlotta, please do it. I'll do anything for you. Word of honour. And anyway, the go-between was also one of the useful tips I read out on the way here. It said you should just send a good mate on **ahead** to check out the situation. Someone you can trust absolutely," she **stressed**.

I thought for a moment. Anke had come up with quite a role for me. I wanted to say no, but then I saw the expectation in her face.

"Please say yes," she urged. "I promise I'll think up something to take care of Natascha. **Cross my heart and hope to die**!"

I nodded.

Anke threw her arms around my neck. "I knew you were a true friend. Here's your toothbrush, by the way. It was lying in my sponge bag."

"So what's the **procedure**?" I asked, taking my toothbrush from her hand. "Should I go up and say you're in love with him?"

Anke was **appalled** and shook her head. "No, he mustn't find that out yet. You just have to get into conversation with him, find out his name and what he likes, music and stuff like that. And

---

sink – Waschbecken; ahead – voraus; to stress – betonen; Cross my heart and hope to die. – Versprochen ist versprochen und wird nicht gebrochen.; procedure – Vorgehensweise; appalled – entsetzt

then you **rave about** me to him. Tell him I come from Hamburg and that I like discos. And tell him about my plan of becoming a model, too ..."

"I don't know if ..."

"Please, Carlotta! Imagine how Natascha will stare when she sees what's going on."

"All right," I said. "Natascha needs to notice the problems she'll have with me. She probably thinks I still play with dolls. I'll show her she'll have to **reckon with** quite different things."

"So you'll do it?" Anke asked to make certain.

"Yes, I've already told you," I reassured her. "Why are you rubbing toothpaste into your face?"

Anke **gave a start**. "I thought it was skin crème. I'm so mixed up. I'm so glad I have you, Carlotta."

A stage was **lowered** from thick rain clouds. I sat in the middle of the audience and applauded, until I noticed that I was the only person clapping. I looked around and saw to my horror that Mum and Natascha were making an **entrance**. They both had green hair and were singing a duet. Then they suddenly noticed Dad and made a rush for him. "Dad!" I wanted to shout, but Mum was shaking my shoulders.

"Ssh," hissed Anke and sat down next to me on the bed. "Be quiet. Stefanie's still asleep. Did you have a bad dream?"

---

to rave about sb. – von jmdm. schwärmen;
to reckon with – rechnen mit;
to give a start – zusammenzucken; to lower – senken;
entrance – *hier:* Auftritt

I nodded. "A real nightmare."

Anke yawned. "You gave me quite a **fright**. Listen, I've thought of something important." She leant towards me and whispered so quietly I could hardly understand what she was saying. "We have to decide how to proceed. We only have a few days here after all, and we don't yet know how long the other class is staying. Imagine them going home today and ..." She couldn't help raising her voice.

"Who's going home?" inquired Stefanie, who had woken up in the meantime. "And what's up with you two? And look at the clock. It's not even half past six!"

"You were snoring so loudly we couldn't sleep any more," said Anke.

Stefanie gave her a mildly **insulted** look. "I can't imagine I snore. Anyway, I'm going to take a shower." She stood up and **trudged** out of the room.

"We have to be careful when Stefanie's here," I said in a low voice. "It would be really embarrassing if she told someone in the class about this. You know what? We should give the guy a name."

"A name?" said Anke blankly. "But he must have one already."

"Sure, but I was thinking of a kind of working name. It would sound less suspicious if someone heard us talking about him."

"Romeo," my friend suggested. "I think Romeo fits best."

---

fright – Schrecken; insulted – beleidigt;
to trudge – stapfen

I **spluttered**, "And you're Juliet, right? You know how *that* story ends."

"Something else then," said Anke, sounding a little hurt. "But I want him to have a nice name."

"Max," I suggested. "He's probably called Max."

"What makes you think that?" Anke gave me a doubting look. "Do you like that name?"

I nodded. "It sounds very nice. Stefanie told me she got two mice for her birthday called Max and Moritz."

"Mice!" gulped Anke. "I think perhaps another name would be better."

But we couldn't think of another name that was good enough, and when I made it clear to Anke that we were talking about a code name, she finally agreed.

"And do you know what the next step is?"

I nodded. "I've had an idea. I had a think about where we could see him for sure. And that's probably breakfast. So I'll sit down next to him and start up a conversation, and the rest will follow on from there."

Anke looked at me in admiration. "You're doing it just like my mother always says. Don't wait for your prince to come, but take the initiative. Carlotta, I'll never forget this."

"But there's still a small problem." I laughed when I saw Anke's shocked expression. "No, don't worry, but perhaps you should tell me what Max looks like."

---

to splutter – heraussprudeln

I entered the dining room at quarter past eight.

Anke had felt that, too, was a bad idea. "There are still **plenty of** places free then, and everyone will wonder why Carlotta isn't sitting with our class. It would be ideal if you *had* to sit next to Max because there were no other places left." Anke went into breakfast early, at half past seven, to "check out the situation," as she put it, and to give me some exact information about Max. Her description of him as having dark blond, mid-length hair and looking unbelievable sweet wasn't much use to me.

"Imagine I spoke to the wrong guy," I warned. "You absolutely have to find out what he's wearing."

I stayed in our room, my stomach rumbling, and waited. To pass the time until going down, I drew stick men on a paper napkin with a **felt pen**, but then I had a better idea. I took out Anke's sponge bag and put on **tinted** face crème, dark blue eyeshadow and lipstick.

Unfortunately, I couldn't inspect the finished product more closely because the cleaning lady was in the washroom. When I looked into the pocket mirror, I had found under Anke's pillow, I got a terrible shock at first, until I realised it was an **enlarging** mirror.

At that moment there was a knock on the door. Heike put her head in and called, "Anke says you should come at once. Oh yes, and I'm supposed to give you this note." She looked me over

---

plenty of – jede Menge; felt pen – Filzstift;
tinted – getönt; to enlarge – vergrößern

and was about to say something, but I shoved her out of the door and unfolded the note.

White, blue-and-green check, black, I read, grinning. If Heike had read the note, she wouldn't have been able to **make head or tail of** it. I took three deep breaths, like Jenny always did before a concert. Now for my big entrance.

---

to make head or tail of sth. – aus etw. schlau werden

Oblivious

of everything around me, I went into the dining room. Someone or other said, "Ah, here comes Carlotta. Have you been uncoupled again?" Everyone laughed. I didn't react. Out of the corner of my eye I saw that there were still places left next to Natascha and Mr Dannitzki, and that Andrea was standing up to wave to me. As **inconspicuously** as I could, I half turned to the side and took a swift look at the table near me. For a moment I had the impression everyone was staring at me. Where on earth was this damned Max?

"Carlotta," I could hear Natascha calling. "Come and sit with us!"

I had to **gain** some time. Slowly, I went over to the table where the **modest** breakfast buffet was laid out and took two slices of bread. I could hardly march past all the tables looking for a white T-shirt, a blue-and-green checked shirt and black jeans.

"Carlotta, what's wrong?" Dad's new girlfriend was standing right behind me, and that was my starting signal. I grabbed two **slices** of

---

oblivious – *hier:* blind;
inconspicuous – unauffällig; to gain – gewinnen;
modest – bescheiden; slice – Scheibe, Stück

sausage and a **hunk** of cheese and carried my breakfast past a baffled Natascha to the next-best table. And then I saw him! He was sitting on the long side of the neighbouring table – at least he corresponded to the description on Anke's note – and was spreading jam on a slice of bread.

With an elegant turn, I **dodged** our Maths teacher, who was probably hurrying to help Natascha in her state of shock, to find myself standing directly opposite Max. All the places at his table were taken, of course, but I couldn't take any notice of that.

The boys at the table were astonished when I suddenly squeezed myself onto the bench between them, put two slices of bread, two slices of sausage and a hunk of cheese on the table and said hello. I heard my own voice coming from far away. It sounded high and strange.

I had the feeling that there was a breathless silence throughout the dining room. Everything seemed to be waiting for what I would say next. Nothing mattered any more anyway, and I saw myself putting my hand across the table and heard myself saying, "Hello, I'm Carlotta, and what's your name?"

The boy opposite looked up. Dark brown eyes, a small scar on his chin, I noted to myself. There was still a **deathly hush** all around. The boy swallowed, then took my hand, shook it and said his name was Jannis. Then he let go of my hand. In

---

hunk – dickes Stück; to dodge – ausweichen;
deathly hush – Todesstille

the background I could hear the buzz of chatter. Someone gave a low laugh.

I suddenly felt **wretched**. I'd like to have gathered up my breakfast again and fled to my own class, but somehow I couldn't. Jannis was still looking at me, and for a moment I had the impression he was smiling.

Now you should smile, too, said a voice within me, go on, at least try.

I gave the hunk of cheese in front of me an embarrassed smile and noticed I'd chosen **cheese spread**.

"Do you like cheese spread?" I asked, looking at Jannis. There were little green flashes in his eyes.

"Cheese spread? Not much," he said. "Why do you ask?"

"No reason," I said. No one at the table said a word. Why was I so uncertain all of a sudden? I remembered my mother talking about the "chaos in your head before your entrance," and I felt the same chaos. I had to do something against it.

"My mate loves cheese spread," I said into the silence.

"Hey! Why don't you ask me what kind of cheese I like? My name's Olli, by the way, Kai-Oliver, but all the nice people call me Olli," said the guy next to Jannis, waving at me with both hands.

Everyone around me laughed, including Jan-

---

wretched – elend, mies;
cheese spread – Streichkäse

nis, and I had to laugh as well. "All right, I'm asking," I said and held out my hand to him, too.

"Well, cheese spread is pretty **cheesy**, if you want to know."

"I don't think she *does* want to know," said another boy. "Can't you see that this is the start of something big?" He poked Jannis in the ribs. "Hey, no one's ever been interested in your taste in cheese before. Do you think Carlotta's from a market research institute?"

Jannis shook his head. I had the feeling the situation was getting really embarrassing for him.

"And what's your class doing today?" Olli asked after a while.

"We're going to Dresden," I said. "And you lot?"

Olli was the most talkative of them. Within ten minutes I had found out that the class came from Stuttgart, was going back in three days and had been on a **load of** terrible hikes.

"There's no end to them. Today we can go part of the way by bus, but we have to walk back," Olli complained, pointing to his teacher, who was standing with a whistle at the entrance to the dining room, waving his pupils towards him. "Can you imagine? At least 24 kilometres. He wants to chase us over the fields again. Bye, Carlotta, we have to go."

The class from Stuttgart had hardly disappeared when Anke came and sat down beside me. "You were **fab**, Carlotta, just fab. I don't

---

cheesy – doof; load of – eine Menge;
fab (= fabulous) – toll

know what I'd do without you. You should have seen how the others were staring. Tina almost **fainted**. But tell me what you found out."

It wasn't much, she said disappointedly. And what had I told them about her?

I looked at her in annoyance. "You know what? I make the most **incredible** effort, and you're not even satisfied. Just be happy you know his name now and that you've got three days to get to know him."

"Sorry." She seemed pretty **put out** because she knew full well she needed me. "But you'll still help me, won't you? By the way, you should go over to Natascha. I heard her talking to Danni just now about wanting to speak to you."

"You know, Anke," I said, trying to keep myself from seeming too triumphant, "Natascha is a **pest**. First she gets on my nerves at Dad's house, and then she has to come with us to the youth hostel to play mother **substitute**, and now she probably wants to forbid me from having anything to do with boys. She doesn't know I'm only doing it for you."

"Silly cow," **moaned** Anke. "But you won't let her tell you what to do."

I laughed. "No way, not her. If she wants me, she should come over herself."

---

to faint – ohnmächtig werden;
incredible – unglaublich; put out – *hier:* verärgert;
pest – Nervensäge;
substitute – Ersatz; to moan – klagen

On the way from the dining room to the front door, where our coach to Dresden was waiting, Mr Dannitzki took me to one side. "Well, Carlotta, did you fall into a can of paint this morning?" he asked in a mildly **mocking** tone that immediately became serious again. "Please sit down with Natascha sometime this morning. She'd like to talk to you."

I nodded. I certainly wasn't going to talk to my Maths teacher about my problems with Dad's new girlfriend.

The coach was supposed to leave punctually at nine, but of course some of the class weren't ready, and Natascha ran back and forth like a headless chicken. The driver didn't seem to mind. He had taken off his glasses, crossed his arms over his **belly** and was taking a mid-morning nap. At exactly half past nine he sat up, turned round and **croaked**, "Everyone here?", went into first **gear** and drove off without waiting for an answer.

"We're in luck that everyone really *is* here," I heard Danni saying to Natascha. The two of them were sitting right behind me.

"And in even more luck that he didn't leave at nine o'clock sharp as arranged," she added, laughing quietly. "Or did we arrange half past nine? Never mind, the main thing is we're all in the coach and it isn't raining. Wait a second. Where's he going? We need to turn right for

---

mocking – spottend;
belly – Bauch;
to croak – krächzen; gear – Gang

Dresden." She waved to the front **in a fluster**, calling out, "We should have turned off here."

The coach driver **flicked** the **indicator**, put his foot hard on the brake and turned right. Then he turned around. "Now you listen to me, Miss. There's only one driver and that's me. Got it? And if you don't like it, you can walk, right?"

He indicated left and filtered back into the traffic. In the coach there was silence, apart from some **furtive** giggling. I turned round and saw that Natascha had gone a deep red.

"I'll talk to the man. Or even better, I'll complain right away to his boss," said Mr Dannitzki, all worked up. "We don't have to put up with that kind of treatment. We're paying after all."

Natascha put her hand on his arm. "Don't get annoyed, it isn't worth it. And anyway, he's the boss himself."

I **winked at** Anke next to me, and she grinned back. Natascha would probably never go on a school trip again.

"What's the next step with Jannis?" she whispered. "I was wondering if he might like to become a model, too. And then, just imagine, we could do it together!"

"Yes," I said, looking at her from the side. When I told Dad about Anke's model plans, he had only laughed and said my friend had some big ideas. But perhaps she'd really make it.

---

in a fluster – aufgeregt;
to flick – *hier:* setzen; indicator – *hier:* Blinker;
furtive – verstohlen;
to wink at sb. – jmdm. zuzwinkern

"So? What do you think?"

I shrugged my shoulders. "Anke, I don't know."

"Have you got an idea?"

"Perhaps I'm not **cut out** to be a go-between."

Anke looked at me in consternation. "Oh Carlotta, you're doing great, really, believe me. Of course you couldn't tell him very much about me the first time. I don't mind. You just have to help me out once more. Tell him something about me, and then I'll come past by chance and ..."

"Why have you fallen in love with him, actually?"

Anke shrugged her shoulders. "I don't know. Just think, I've never spoken a word to him and I'm still in love. These things just happen. So, have another go with Jannis, okay?"

I thought about Jannis's brown eyes with their green **flecks** and nodded.

Meanwhile it had begun raining and Mr Dannitzki decided to reorganise the sightseeing programme in Dresden. "You have to be flexible these days," he said. "The weather will be better in the afternoon, perhaps. We'll go to a museum this morning. Some of the ladies may have forgotten their umbrellas and rainwear, or are wearing slippers again, like our own dear Anke, am I right?" He bent forward to inspect Anke's shoes and shook his head **in defeat**. "Aha, silver

---

to be cut out – geeignet sein;
fleck – Fleck;
in defeat – resigniert

today. Goes perfectly with the grey sky. I'm afraid we may have to spend the whole day in the museum."

Anke pulled a face. "How far is it still?"

"It would only take about an hour by the quickest route, but our driver's going the long way around," Natascha explained.

"Perhaps he wants to show us the beauty of Saxony in heavy rain," laughed our Maths teacher, pointing out of the window. "We've been travelling through these woods for at least five minutes."

The coach stopped and I heard Natascha giggling nervously behind me. "Have I said something wrong again, and too loudly as well?" she whispered to Mr Dannitzki.

The doors opened and the driver turned around to us. "If I might ask you to leave the bus, ladies and gentlemen. I have other things to do today after all."

We looked at each other helplessly – we had imagined Dresden quite differently. Mr Dannitzki had stood up and gone to the front. "Why are you stopping here? What's all this?"

"What's all this?" The driver had folded his arms and was looking indignantly over his glasses. "One thing I know for sure. No more school outings. They only bring disaster!"

"I'd like to know why you're stopping here," said Mr Dannitzki, putting on a typical senior teacher's voice. "If you would kindly give me a reasonable explanation."

The man pointed to a small sign in the car park. "Ölmüsser Höhe! Do you understand?" He was talking to our Maths teacher as if he were hard of hearing.

"I don't mind if you put us off **on the outskirts** of Dresden. We can take the public transport from there," **blustered** Danni. "But we had a telephone agreement that you would take us to the city centre."

"Dresden?" The man laughed. "Dresden my foot. You **persuaded** me yesterday to drive to the Ölmüsser Höhe because you wanted to walk back with your class. Which, by the way, is a completely idiotic thing to do. But that's what you wanted. So if you'd all get off please. This is a regular bus and I have to be at the **district nursing home** at ten."

"I think we got on the wrong bus," said Tina as we watched it drive away from the car park a minute later.

Anke applauded mockingly, "Bravo Tina, got it in one."

Natascha gave her a look of displeasure. "Please Anke, we can do without arguments at the moment. And we don't need to find out who got on the wrong bus first. The fact is ..." She looked around in silence.

"The fact is that we're somewhere in the middle of the countryside, that the class from ..."

"Stuttgart," I called out.

"... wherever, from Stuttgart, are sitting in our coach and that we have to get back somehow,"

---

on the outskirts – am Stadtrand;
to bluster – blaffen; to persuade – überreden;
district – Bezirks-; nursing home – Altenheim

explained Danni and received an **howl** of **indignation**.

"In this rain?"

"Didn't the man say something about regular buses?" Natascha looked around uncertainly, but there was no bus stop to be seen.

"And why didn't he at least take us as far as that nursing home?" asked Christine, **draping** a plastic bag over her head like a turban.

"Because he's an idiot," said Stefanie, shaking her head.

Danni nodded. "One shouldn't say so, but in this case that's exactly right. But still, ladies, moaning won't help. We'll just go on the hike today that we were going to go on tomorrow." After three steps he took hold of his back. "I'm afraid I really *am* too old for the twist."

"And we're too young for being marched around like this," grumbled Heike.

Danni laughed and promised us a video evening – and even a disco, if the hostel wardens had no **objection** – to **make up for** things. The disco was Anke's suggestion, and I knew why. Despite her sandals the rain didn't seem to **bother** her at all. She had only one thing on her mind – Jannis – and was making plans for the future.

"And what if he isn't in love with you?" I asked.

---

howl – Aufschrei;
indignation – Empörung; to drape – drapieren;
objection – Einwand;
to make up for sth. – etw. wiedergutmachen;
to bother – stören

Anke laughed. "I think he already *is* in love with me," she said. "At least he was standing in the dining room doorway this morning when I sat down next to you, and I saw his look. It was so sweet."

I shrugged my shoulders. "Well, if you say so."

The rain had become less heavy in the meantime, it was only drizzling, and Danni was explaining natural phenomena yet again to a hard **core** of Maths losers who had gathered around him. I trudged behind the others on my own for a while, when I noticed that Natascha, who had been walking with a group in front of me, was slowing her pace. I knew at once that she was waiting for an opportunity to talk to me. I slowed down; Natascha, too. In the end, she just stood and waited for me.

"What a disaster," she said.

I didn't say a word. I just kept on walking as if she wasn't there.

"I wanted to talk to you!" She tried hard to stay friendly. "You put on quite a lot of make-up this morning."

I pulled a face. Natascha was probably behaving the way she thought my mother would. Don't make me laugh! Jenny would never mind me putting on make-up.

"So? Does it bother you?" I asked.

Natascha laughed softly. "No, of course not. I can't tell you what to do. But to be honest, I don't think you were very well made up. The lipstick

---

core – Kern

was too bright and the foundation too dark. You know, the art of make-up is to look as if you aren't wearing any."

At first I wanted to say something **cheeky**, but unfortunately, I knew intuitively she was right. It was an awful feeling. What on earth had Jannis thought of me? I turned to one side and was glad it began to rain again just at that moment. I'd never let Dad's new girlfriend have the triumph of seeing me cry. I could feel I was close to tears.

"I'll give you a few tips, if you like," she called after me as I ran to the front to Anke, my mate.

"What's wrong?" asked Anke. "What did Natascha want?"

"The silly cow wants to forbid me to talk to Jannis again," I lied.

Anke gave me a horrified look. "**You're kidding**."

"No, I'm not," I lied. "She's **out of the ark**."

"We have to do something about this," said Anke decisively. "Otherwise she'll ruin my entire future."

But we couldn't think of anything workable. I kept hearing Natascha's voice in my mind. "Lipstick too bright. Foundation too dark." She had told me I looked **dreadful**, and the worst thing was – I could feel she was right.

"You're no fun," said Stefanie, giving me a worried look. "Are you getting ill?"

---

cheeky – frech;
You're kidding. – Du machst Witze.;
to be out of the ark – altmodisch sein;
dreadful – furchtbar

"I'm just fed up with **traipsing** around in the rain," I said.

Jannis must have thought I was totally out of order going up to his table covered in **warpaint**. I **unobtrusively** wiped the rest of the make-up off my face with a paper handkerchief and looked in horror at the mixture of dark blue, pink and dark brown. Ridiculous. Exactly. I had looked like a ridiculous figure in a comedy. No wonder the boys at Jannis's table had stared at me.

"Carlotta, are your father and Natascha half married already?" Andrea suddenly wanted to know.

I shook my head. "What gives you *that* idea?"

"My mother said a good friend of your father was coming with us," said Tina with an inquisitive look. "Do you think they'll get married soon? That would be great for you as well. Natascha's really all right."

"I want to tell you something," I said in a low voice. "But keep it to yourselves, okay?"

Andrea and Tina nodded **eagerly**, and I knew that the whole class would hear about it within half an hour.

"Keep it to yourselves," I repeated. I made a dramatic pause and they stared at me with **undisguised** curiosity. "Natascha is a sort of **housekeeper**."

"Your housekeeper?" asked Andrea.

---

to traipse – latschen; warpaint – Kriegsbemalung; unobtrusive – unauffällig; eager – eifrig; undisguised – unverschleiert; housekeeper – Haushälter/-in

I nodded. "Yes, she helps out from time to time. She cooks quite good noodles with chocolate sauce and little things like that."

The two of them were amazed. They made a few trivial remarks and then joined the others to pass on the news. For a moment I thought about saying, "Oh, it was just a joke," but I decided to let it be. Natascha was trying to take my father away from me, and I had to be **ruthless**.

Anke gave me a questioning look. "You're feeling bad, aren't you? Just because of Natascha!"

I nodded. But Natascha wasn't the reason. *I* was thinking about Jannis the whole time, too.

"Do you think your parents might get together again? Then the problem would solve itself. Can't you give things a helping hand in that direction?"

"I don't think I want to give them a helping hand," I said. "My parents just don't go together. They're both really nice on their own, but when they're together ... there's an endless **row**. Last year, just before the divorce ..." I hesitated for a moment, and Anke interrupted.

"I know. Just don't ask what it was like between my mum and dad. If my mother wanted to go to the cinema, my father wanted to watch something on telly. They didn't have a single day without an argument." She kicked a stone angrily to one side. "At some point I told them to split up, I couldn't **take it** any more. And they did.

---

ruthless – rücksichtslos;
row – Streit; to take it – *hier:* etw. ertragen

And I'm going to make sure that when I have a relationship, it'll be with a guy who has the same interests as me. Otherwise it won't work, know what I mean?"

We reached the youth hostel at around half past three. Danni had phoned the wardens while we were hiking, so that we could at least get some lunch. "You can have the afternoon off for hiking so well," he said **in praise**. "And the video has been repaired. We'll watch a nice film this evening."

"Perhaps one of Stephen King's," suggested Franziska. "They're very nice films."

"I don't know them, but whatever you want," said Danni. "If you've got one with you."

Franziska grinned at us, and Natascha pulled our Maths teacher discretely to one side. She was probably explaining to him about the 'nice' film. At any rate, after a while Danni said it might be better if he showed a film he knew. And there were plenty of charming **parlour games**, and we could also play cards in the evening. Some of the class grumbled, of course, and Danni got all strict and began **sounding off** that watching videos wasn't a God-given right.

I didn't care either way. I had other worries. Firstly, I hoped that I hadn't stood out to Jannis *too* negatively with my breakfast make-up. Secondly, I didn't want the thing about the 'house-

---

in praise – lobend;
parlour game – Gesellschaftsspiel;
to sound off – die Meinung sagen, predigen

keeper' to get around too much – Dad would really **lay into** me for that – and thirdly, Anke was going on at me the whole time with new ideas about how she could meet Jannis at last.

In the end, we agreed that I would wait in the lobby for the Stuttgart class to come back from their **unintended** trip to Dresden and then **get** Jannis **involved in** conversation. Anke would wait outside by the horses, and I was supposed to bring him outside – after telling him a few things about her – and leave the two of them alone on some **pretext** after a minute or two.

"I'll go outside as soon as I see you talking," said Anke. "Just don't forget what you're supposed to tell him about me."

"Should I take a **crib** with me, or a **prompter**?" I asked. "You have to leave things to me."

---

to lay into sb. – jmdm. die Hölle heiß machen;
unintended – unbeabsichtigt;
to get sb. involved in – jmdn. verwickeln in;
pretext – Vorwand; crib – Spickzettel;
prompter – Souffleur/Souffleuse

The bus

carrying Jannis' class got back just after five, and I positioned myself on a bench near reception. He was bound to see me here. I had carefully washed my face again, all traces of **foundation**, eyeshadow and lipstick had disappeared, and I noticed how nervous I was. I planned to tell him about Anke almost immediately – how much she liked animals, above all horses – and suggest going to the field behind the hostel to have a look at the foals.

"But don't **blurt it out**," Anke had warned me, "otherwise it won't sound natural."

"I know how to handle it," I had said, pretending to be cool.

But when Jannis came up to me with a wave, **my heart was in my mouth**.

"Poor things," was his greeting. "You've been hiking, right? From Ölmüsser Höhe to here. 24.7 kilometres, Jessing told us."

"Jessing?"

"Our teacher. Can you imagine, he put us on

---

foundation – Grundierung;
to blurt sth. out – sofort sagen;
My heart was in my mouth. – Das Herz schlug mir bis zum Hals.

the bus that was waiting for you. The driver wanted to say something, but he cut him off. Once we were in Dresden, he was really surprised that Ölmüsser Höhe was in the middle of a city. You should have seen his face." Jannis laughed out loud. "He looked **pathetic**."

"And what did you do the whole time in Dresden?" I asked. He had long eyelashes, I noticed, almost as long as the ones Jenny stuck on when she had a performance.

"What are you staring at? Is something wrong?" asked Jannis. "Has Olli stuck a **price tag** on my **forehead** again or something?"

"No," I said. "Everything's fine. Tell me what you did."

"Well, of course Jessing wasn't prepared for Dresden, so he let us have a look at the city on our own. I discovered a great surfing shop."

"Internet?"

Jannis laughed. "No, no, not Internet. Real surfing. It's not really in any more, but I think it's great. If I ever have a lot of money, I want to go to Hawaii. That's where the best waves in the world are. Have you ever been surfing?"

I shook my head. I didn't want to admit that I was a bit afraid of water and last year only managed to jump off the three-metre board because the Sports teacher was down below **threatening** me with an E in my **report**. "No," I said, "not yet. But I'd like to try it."

---

pathetic – *hier*: bescheuert;
price tag – Preisschild; forehead – Stirn;
to threaten – drohen; report – Zeugnis

"There are youth hostels by the sea where we could have gone surfing, but all Jessing can do is go hiking and that's why he chose Saxony. A few of the guys in our class wanted to go to a motor race, and he almost fainted."

"And you? Did you want to as well?"

Jannis nodded enthusiastically. "I'm interested in sports cars. Have you seen that great car behind the youth hostel? A yellow Lamborghini! Wicked! I'd like to have a drive in it."

I realised too late that now I could actually tell him about Anke, and how she'd recently had a lift in this car.

"We wanted to go to Berlin," I said instead. "But then our teacher broke her leg, and Danni – that's our Maths teacher – is afraid of cities. So we ended up in this **dump**. And the worst thing is that Natascha had to come, too ..."

And I told him the whole story. About Jenny and Dad and Natascha and the noodles with chocolate sauce, everything. Jannis listened and occasionally laughed, and at the bit about the noodles with chocolate sauce he shook his head in disbelief. Next door the gong sounded for the evening meal, but I just went on talking and Jannis didn't seem to be in any hurry to go into the dining room.

"Carlotta!" Stefanie was standing in front of me. "Here you are!"

I jumped up **guiltily**.

---

dump – *hier:* Loch;
guilty – schuldbewusst

Jannis stood up, too. "I have to go and eat, or Jessing will give me aggro," he said. "Bye."

"What are you doing here?" asked Stefanie. "Anke's standing around in the field, freezing. She's waiting for someone called Jannis. Is that the guy you were just talking to? What's going on here anyway?"

"Anke asked me to talk to Jannis," I said. How much did Stefanie in fact know about the whole thing? "And anyway, it's her own fault if she's freezing. I told her just now to put warm socks on, but please, if she's too **vain** to take my advice, she can't complain about being cold."

"Anke told me she was in love with the guy," said Stefanie. "And you were supposed to send him out to her. Why didn't you?"

"I had to gain his **trust** first. You don't seriously think that after three sentences I can **go into raptures** to a boy I don't know **about** my phenomenally fantastic friend who **happens to** be standing around outside in a field, and he just runs outside and ..." I shook my head. Stefanie had to see what I meant.

"A bit more than three sentences, I think." Stefanie didn't give up easily. "After you'd been chatting for a while, don't you think you could have found an opportunity to go outside with him?"

---

vain – eitel;
trust – Vertrauen;
to go into raptures about – in Begeisterung ausbrechen über;
to happen to do sth. – zufällig etw. tun

I shook my head. "No, that's what I mean. The field was a ridiculous idea. Jannis is allergic to horses. He might have had an allergic reaction or something, and we'd have gone to all that trouble for nothing."

Stefanie still looked a little **mistrustful**. "Tell that to Anke."

Of course I told Anke something about "building up trust". It seemed to make sense to her or, at any rate, put her in a better mood.

"If we go to the dining room now, we might still meet him," I suggested, but Anke wasn't in any particular hurry.

The next act needed careful planning, she said, and I had to tell her in detail what I had found out about Jannis.

"I have news, too, by the way." Anke looked at me uncertainly for a moment, as if she was wondering whether to say anything at all. Then she laughed. "There's a party tonight. It's Heike's birthday tomorrow and she's celebrating from ten onwards."

"Why wait till ten?" I asked, stifling a yawn. Today's hike had **done me in**.

"The party's probably starting that late so Danni and Natascha won't know it's happening. And guess what, Heike has invited the Stuttgarters." Anke beamed. "I guess Jannis will be there, too. It's my big chance."

I swallowed. "Did Heike invite you?"

---

mistrustful – misstrauisch;
to do sb. in – jmdn. fertig machen

"Sure. She couldn't not. I heard about it by chance just now and said, 'Oh great, how nice,' so she *had* to invite me. But I don't think she really wanted to." Anke laughed. "Perhaps she'll think Jannis is sweet, too, who knows. Anyway, I'll talk to him immediately about surfing and the Lamborghini, and then it'll be difficult for Heike to get into conversation with him."

"Well, have fun," I said. "Are you coming in to eat?"

"What do you mean, have fun?" Anke looked at me **quizzically**. "Don't you want to come?"

I shrugged my shoulders. "I haven't been invited. And I haven't got a present either."

"None of us have presents," said Anke. "Heike arranged the party at such short notice. But we ought to bring her some of our supplies, as a kind of entry ticket. Of course you're invited. Stefanie's going, too. Or do you want a written invitation?"

"Yes," I'd like to have said, "I do." But then I had to laugh and said I'd have to think about it.

"We should bring something from the evening meal, above all cheese. Heike wants to make a cheese platter. We could **donate** the rest of our pretzels." Anke thought for a moment. "Do you think I could bring my rucksack downstairs and fill it with stuff from the dining room, or would people notice?"

"Of course people would notice, and Danni would become suspicious. Leave your rucksack

---

quizzical – fragend; to donate – spenden

here," said Stefanie, who had just entered the room.

"Are you going to just carry the cheese up in your hands?" asked Anke. "People will *really* notice that. Say something, Carlotta. You look as if it had nothing to do with you. Anyway, you two can do what you like. I'm taking my rucksack and that's that."

We could have saved ourselves the argument. That evening there was **lentils** with sausages and stewed fruit for **pudding**.

"Well, we're not going to the party for the brilliant food," said Anke, shoving her empty rucksack inconspicuously under the table.

Almost everyone in our class – except for Tina and Agnes, who weren't in the know – was yawning so noticeably that Mr Dannitzki, who had been intending to play parlour games with us, said with a laugh that he'd never seen so many **clapped out** old wrecks and we ought to be off to bed.

Anke and I went to our room. "It's my big chance this evening," she said in an undertone, laying her pullovers out on the bed. "Do you think I should wear the blue one or the striped one?"

"I think the blue one's better," I said. "Do you think anything will happen this evening?"

Anke put on her blue pullover and stuffed the striped one back into the cupboard. "I hope so.

---

lentil – Linse;
pudding – Nachtisch;
clapped out – erschöpft

Oh Carlotta, I'm incredibly nervous. Have you ever been in love?"

"Me? No, not really," I said, looking at my clothes. What should I wear to the birthday party?

"You can have my white sweatshirt, if you want," offered Anke. "It'll look good with your black hair." She filled two **beakers** with apple juice. "To Jannis. **Keep your fingers crossed** that things go well."

"To Jannis," I said, feeling the blood rush to my cheeks.

Fortunately, Stefanie came through the door at that moment, proudly showing us a **bunch** of flowers. "I picked them at the **edge** of the woods. They'll be our present. What do you think?"

"Lovely," said Anke approvingly. "You know what? I'm going to set the alarm for half past nine and have a sleep till then. When the alarm rings, I'll still have enough time to put my make-up on and at ten I'll be in a real party mood."

Ten minutes later Anke seemed to be asleep. Stefanie was writing her diary. For a while I stared out into the darkened garden and then lay down on the bed. I was tired, but I couldn't go to sleep. At least that was what I thought.

"Carlotta, Carlotta!" I could hear Stefanie's voice next to me. "Please wake up."

I sat up with a start. I hadn't *been* asleep.

She shone her pocket torch around and held

---

beaker – Zahnputzbecher;
to keep one's fingers crossed – die Daumen drücken;
bunch – Strauß; edge – Rand

Anke's alarm clock up to my face. I had to **screw up** my eyes to be able to see anything at all by such a **faint** light. "Half past twelve? Stefanie, that can't be right. The party starts at ten."

She nodded. "It started at ten, but probably without us. Absolutely without us. I've told Anke twice already to change the batteries in her alarm clock, but she keeps forgetting. What a **letdown**. Shall we wake her?"

I thought for a moment. Then I shook my head. "You and I will go to Heike's and see what's happening. Just think, Jannis could be sitting holding hands with the birthday girl. Anke would get the shock of her life. We'll check first. We can still come and fetch her. If we can wake her up at all."

Anke had rolled herself up under the bedcovers like a **hedgehog**. She didn't even wake up when I opened the creaking cupboard door to take out a thick pullover.

"You're right," said Stefanie. "Let's go alone first and fetch her later."

There was no light in the long corridor and we couldn't hear anything anywhere. We crept up to the door of Heike's room and listened. It was extremely quiet for a big party, I thought. I pressed down the door handle quietly – and was amazed. The street lamp directly outside the window illuminated seven sleeping classmates, some of whom were snoring softly.

---

to screw up – *hier:* zusammenkneifen;
faint – schwach; letdown – Reinfall;
hedgehog – Igel

"Great party," whispered Stefanie. "Wonderful atmosphere here."

Heike woke and sat up. "What are you doing here?" she asked sleepily. "What time is it anyway?"

We sat down on her bed. "I thought there was a party here," I said. "Congratulations, by the way."

"Oh yes, my birthday," she mumbled. "The party was a **dead loss**. It started off nicely. There were 16 of us here and the Stuttgarters were going to come at half past ten." She shook her head. "And then that guy Olli, the one who's always **fooling around**, actually managed to carry up the big glass vase with **branches** in it from downstairs. But the idiot **tripped** and ... Didn't the noise wake you up?"

"We've got the broom cupboard at the back round the corner," I explained. "It's probably **soundproof**."

"At any rate, Tina and Agnes were woken up and found out that something was going on here without them. They were angry and made such a loud fuss that first Natascha, then Danni and finally Mr Jessing came – and that was the end of the party."

She yawned and pulled up the bedcovers. "Nice you came round. Good night."

We could see light through the narrow **gap**

---

a dead loss – eine totale Pleite;
to fool around – herumalbern; branch – Zweig;
to trip – stolpern; soundproof – schalldicht;
gap – Spalt, Lücke

under the door to our room. "Did you leave the light on?" I asked in astonishment.

Stefanie shrugged her shoulders and opened the door quietly.

Anke was sitting on the **windowsill**, her arms folded, her face swollen from crying. "I hope the party was nice," she **sobbed**.

I shook my head, and Stefanie took a step towards Anke.

"Keep back or I'll bite," she snapped. "You're wonderful friends. Go to the party and leave me here. You're **way out of line**, both of you. I'm moving out tomorrow. To Tina and Agnes, if I have to. They'd never **deceive** me like you two." Again she sobbed.

By half past two she had finally calmed down enough to more or less believe what we said. But she insisted on going with us to Heike and have her confirm the whole story. Nothing seemed to surprise Heike any more. She accepted our birthday wishes for the second time that night, and once again told us about her **dismal** party. This time she puffed up the story a bit more: Natascha had had a thick **layer** of night crème on her face, and this had given Olli such a shock that he screamed, and this was what had woken his teacher. But the fact was that the party

---

windowsill – Fensterbrett;
to sob – schluchzen;
to be way out of line – hinterhältig/falsch sein;
to deceive – hintergehen; dismal – trostlos;
layer – Schicht

hadn't happened at all, so Anke hadn't missed a thing.

We said goodbye to Heike, promising not to show up again that night, and in the corridor walked right into Mr Dannitzki.

"If I see anything else tonight that even faintly reminds me of my schoolgirls, I'll **take early retirement** and **breed** sheep," he threatened. "At least they don't **stagger** through youth hostels at night."

The rest of the night I hardly slept. I had fallen in love with Jannis, that was clear. And not just a little. I didn't just think he was quite nice, no, I was totally in love. When I closed my eyes, I saw his face in front of me, the little scar on his chin, the crown of his hair slightly to the right. And his eyes: dark brown with little green flashes. It was enough to drive you mad. I **tossed and turned** and tried to go to sleep, but it was pointless.

I heard Anke doing the same thing in the bed below me. "Carlotta," she whispered, "are you awake?"

I didn't reply. I didn't want to talk to Anke just at the moment. I couldn't help having fallen in love with Jannis, of all people. I had only wanted to help Anke. But you can't do anything about feelings, as Jenny always says, and suddenly I knew how right she was. On the other hand, if I showed I'd fallen in love with Jannis, I could forget Anke as a friend.

---

to take early retirement – in Vorruhestand gehen; to breed – züchten; to stagger – *hier:* schleichen; to toss and turn – sich hin- und herwerfen

I rolled back onto my other side.

Dear God, I said silently, I'll make you an offer. I'll give up Jannis for Anke's sake, and you make sure that Natascha gives up Dad or vice versa. Either way they have to separate. I'm making a real sacrifice here.

I sniffled a little into my pillow, and then I thought that my offer would only count if Dad and Natascha separated soon – within the next two weeks – and then I felt better and fell asleep.

"I've decided I have to solve the Jannis problem myself," I heard Anke saying to Stefanie as I woke up. "I'll sit down at his table today. I can't wait till I'm a grandmother." Decisively she **slapped on** a ton of light blue eyeshadow and pink lipstick. "There, how do I look?"

Stefanie shrugged. "I don't know. I like you better without."

Anke turned to me. "So, what do *you* think?"

I **gulped**. Anke had overdone it. She looked as if she was going to a carnival. I must have looked just like that the day before.

"Come on, tell me what you think."

I thought about what I'd promised last night: I'd give up Jannis for Anke's sake. Then Dad and Natascha would separate and …

"What are you staring at? Aren't you feeling well?" Anke put her hand to my forehead. "I bet you've got a temperature."

"Rubbish. I haven't got a temperature at all.

---

to slap on – draufklatschen;
gulped – schlucken

But I think Stefanie's right. You've got too much make-up on."

Stefanie looked at me uncertainly, then shook her head. "I've changed my mind. It doesn't look too bad."

Anke beamed at her. "There you go. Shall I do your face like this sometime?"

Stefanie grinned awkwardly and said yes, sometime, but not at the moment because she was really hungry and why didn't she and I go down to the dining room?

"And what about you, Anke?" I asked.

Anke was brushing her long, blond hair, which she **tossed** behind her **with a flourish**. "My entrance comes later. Leave things to me," she said, pushing us out of the room.

Stefanie and I marched to the dining room in silence. Quite an angry silence, at least on her side. That's how it felt to me. **On no account** should I get an opportunity to talk to Jannis, that was her aim.

"Are you angry?" she asked.

"No, why?"

"You look so **offended**, as if I'd upset you."

I laughed. "Of course you've upset me. You're behaving as if I wanted to get between Anke and her precious Jannis. Are you in love with him yourself, or what?"

Stefanie went bright red. She could hardly control her anger. "You're totally out of order."

---

to toss – werfen; with a flourish – mit Schwung;
on no account – unter keinen Umständen;
offended – beleidigt

"Sorry," I said, "I didn't mean it like that." Then I opened the dining-room door.

Stefanie sat down at the first available place, next to Tina.

I looked around. The place next to Jannis was free, and I imagined he was saving it for me. I was about to be pleased, but then I remembered what I had decided that night and with a sigh I went over to where Mr Dannitzki and Natascha were sitting.

Dad's new girlfriend was in a good mood. She was listening with interest to Heike telling her about how she'd taken the lead role in a primary-school play – **The Princess and the Pea**. At least she was pretending to be interested. And when Agnes, who was the second-worst creep in the class after Tina, said she'd like to be an actress, too, she didn't laugh out loud as you might expect, but said quite seriously that it wasn't all that difficult and you didn't have to be able to do anything very much really.

"So what *can* you do?" asked Agnes eagerly.

I started feeling uncomfortable because I had the stupid feeling that she was going to start on about Natascha's supposed job as a housekeeper.

Natascha laughed. "All I can do is act."

"But you work as a housekeeper for Carlotta's father," said Agnes, looking at her in astonishment. "You have to be able to do a thing or two for that." For a moment Natascha seemed a little

---

The Princess and the Pea – Die Prinzessin auf der Erbse

hesitant, but then she pulled herself together. "Yes, I do that now and then, and sometimes I cook Carlotta's favourite dishes, don't I, Carlotta? But really, all I can do is act."

Mr Dannitzki raised his cup as if he wanted to make a toast to her. "That you can, Ms Lewin. You're an outstanding actress." And as he said it, he laughed as I've never heard a Maths teacher laugh before.

Natascha looked over to me and smiled. I smiled back. The poor thing didn't know she was about to be separated from Dad. She might as well think herself in safety, or at least be surprised that I wasn't being so unfriendly to her all of a sudden.

"Move up a bit." Stefanie squeezed in beside me. "Sorry about just now. But the whole situation was stupid in a way," she whispered. "Hey, can you go and look for Anke? She wanted to come down after us, but I can't see her anywhere. I hope she isn't **in a huff** again about last night."

What I should have said now was "Go and look for her yourself if you're so worried," but I didn't want to be mean. And anyway, Stefanie must have been afraid I'd sit next to Jannis in a flash once she'd left the dining room.

"All right," I said, and on the way out stuffed a piece of cake into my mouth that I'd **nicked** from someone's plate.

As I went past Jannis's table, Olli signalled

---

in a huff – beleidigt; to nick – stibitzen

with both arms and called out something. A few people laughed, but not Jannis. I saw exactly what was going on, although I pretended not to be looking at him. I'd have liked to sit down next to him and tell him everything, but, firstly, I'd promised that night to give him up and, secondly, I was sure Stefanie was watching me with **eagle** eyes.

I opened the door to our room noisily, but **stopped short**. I had expected to see Anke standing in front of the wardrobe or **armed** with her make-up mirror, but she was lying **motionless** on the bed. Her eyes were closed and her hands were folded over her chest.

"Anke, what's wrong? Are you feeling ill? Are you dead, or what?" She ignored me. She was mumbling something to herself over and over again. I bent over her cautiously and held my breath until I could understand what she was saying: "I'm strong, I'm beautiful, I'm brave. I'll sit down next to Jannis. I'm strong, I'm ..."

She let her hands fall. "Damn, I've lost the thread." She sat up **reluctantly**. When she saw me staring, she grinned. "Don't look so shocked. I was doing some self-hypnosis. It's supposed to help with **stage fright** before exams and stuff like that. I thought it could be useful for this, too."

"And do you feel strong and beautiful now? And brave?"

---

eagle – Adler;
to stop short – abrupt stehen bleiben;
armed – bewaffnet; motionless – bewegungslos;
reluctant – widerwillig; stage fright – Lampenfieber

She thought for a moment. "I don't know. You interrupted me. I'd probably have needed two or three more minutes for it to take effect properly. But now it'll have to do."

At the door she turned round briefly. "How do I look?"

I nodded at her.

She made the victory sign, blew me a kiss, said, "Thanks for preparing the ground," and swished out.

But Anke

had nothing but bad luck that morning. "First," she told me later, "Jannis went out of the dining room just as I was going in. And I'd even have had something to talk about. His right hand was in a bandage, and I could have asked him what had happened. Second, our beloved Maths teacher came up to me and gave me an awful lecture on hiking shoes and sandals." She pulled a face. "My self-hypnosis earlier *was* quite helpful. Otherwise I'd have freaked. At any rate, I had to sit with him and Natasha. I wasn't allowed to have any coffee either. Coffee is apparently only for adults, according to Danni, and for us there was **camomile** and peppermint tea." Anke shook her head. "Camomile and peppermint tea, ugh! And Jannis had already left." She sobbed. "That was the worst thing this morning."

"Come on, Anke, don't get worked up," Stefanie comforted her. "There's some good news. The hike to the weird thing Danni couldn't find recently has been cancelled. At least for this afternoon."

"Why's that?"

"Danni **has a soft spot for** Natascha." Anke

---

camomile – Kamille; to have a soft spot for sb. – für jmdn. eine Schwäche haben

grinned. "They're so sweet, the two of them. Natascha mentioned that she'd got a terrible blister from our marathon from the Ölmüsser Höhe to here yesterday and she could hardly walk. And straight away Danni said we wouldn't have a tiring programme today. Can you imagine? I think Danni is in love with Natascha."

"But he's married. Can you seriously imagine someone falling in love with a Maths teacher? And apart from that he's at least twice as old as she is," I said **doubtfully**. "Natascha gave Danni quite a funny look in his walking boots and red socks and that weird hat he wears for hiking."

"Who knows where love's arrows strike?" said Anke mysteriously.

I wondered if that was perhaps the reward for me giving up Jannis. Yes, perhaps it really was. Danni and Natascha fall madly in love, Danni leaves his wife, gets a divorce and marries Natascha. Then Dad would finally be rid of her.

"We should write some postcards home," said Stefanie, interrupting my thoughts. "Anke and I have already bought some at reception. They also sell stamps, and you can hand in the cards once they're written. That's a real service, don't you think?" She pulled a handful of cards out of her pocket. "Here, look! Erdmannsweiler three times, for my grandparents, my **godmother** and my parents, and this one ..."

"Okay, okay," interrupted Anke impatiently and turned to me. "If you get some, could you bring me three stamps, too?"

---

doubtful – zweifelnd; godmother – Patentante

I nodded, and in quite a good mood I went to reception. Perhaps Danni really was in love with Natascha. She was quite pretty after all. Perhaps Natascha had realised she had no future with Dad. She didn't have to marry our Maths teacher right away. The main thing was for her to keep her fingers off Dad.

There was no one at reception. I looked into the dining room and said to the cleaning lady that I wanted to buy some postcards and stamps.

"I can't get away at the moment," said the woman. "But just go on in. The door's **ajar**. Choose the cards you want and put the money in the **till**. The cards cost 50 cents and it's obvious how much the stamps are."

I hesitated over four different postcards. Should I take the youth hostel at **twilight** or the view of Erdmannsweiler? I turned one of the cards over, read *Kleinkögendorf*, put it down, turned over the next one and then stopped short. The card must have got into the pile by mistake. It had already been written. The address seemed familiar to me, and I knew at once who the sender was without **deciphering** the rather **illegible** handwriting.

My dear Paul, I read, my face burning, *We have been separated now for 13 hours, which seems an eternity to me. Everything is quite nice here. There are a few* **minor** *difficulties with C.,*

---

ajar – angelehnt;
till – Kasse; twilight – Abenddämmerung;
to decipher – entziffern; illegible – unleserlich;
minor – kleinere

but I think things will be all right. Mr D. is charming. I think he sees his daughter in me. Then there was a scrawl that was impossible to read – probably a thousand kisses, I thought bitterly – and **beneath** it *Natascha*.

Dad was never going to get this card, never. I folded it up and stuck it in my trouser pocket.

"So, have you chosen any?" asked the cleaning lady, who had meanwhile finished in the dining room, giving me a searching look. "Or don't you like them?"

"No, I do really," I said quickly and grabbed the first cards I could see.

She counted them carefully, wrote *Postcards 4 x € 0.50* on a piece of white cardboard and put the note and my two-euro coin on top of the till. "It's actually the boss's job, but she can't be everywhere at once. And anyway, she's got enough to worry about at the moment," she added when she saw my face. "We have to keep things in order here. I'm curious to see if they'll catch that hooligan. Have you heard anything, perhaps?"

"No," I said. I didn't know what the woman was talking about and I didn't much care.

"At any rate, he must have given himself quite an injury when he drove the car into the **ditch**. Serves him right. Taking the boss's car, **jump-starting** it and driving off. At half past five this morning. And then running away." She shook

---

beneath – darunter;
ditch – Graben;
to jump-start – kurzschließen/anschieben

her head in **indignation**. "We never used to have that kind of thing."

"Do you mean the yellow sports car? The one behind the building?" I asked.

The woman nodded. "If they catch the **fellow**, he'll be in trouble. I don't know what you get for car theft and causing an accident, but it'll certainly be a couple of years."

Vague thoughts came into my head. What had Jannis said? "That yellow Lamborghini! Wicked!" And then the hand injury Anke had told me about. "Shit," I heard myself saying. "He's got himself into trouble!"

I looked around with a start. Hopefully no one had heard me. What could I do? I didn't want Jannis to go to prison for a few years.

I stared uncertainly at the cards in my hand. It was clear to me I had to solve one thing after another. First Natascha's card to Dad. I locked myself in the **loo** and took the card out of my jeans with trembling hands. No, I hadn't been mistaken. Natascha was longing for Dad and her tone was pretty **amorous**. On the other hand the card was from the day before yesterday, and perhaps Natascha had realised what she really felt for Mr Dannitzki by now.

Don't kid yourself, Carlotta, I said to myself back in our room. Dad and Natascha are in love, and Mr Dannitzki loves his wife.

The door opened slowly. Anke and Stefanie

---

indignation – Empörung, Ärger;
fellow – Kerl; loo – Klo;
amorous – verliebt

were staring at me as if I were a ghost. "What took you so long?" asked Anke in a worried voice. "You've gone all pale. Aren't you feeling well?"

"You left the cards at reception, by the way. The cleaning lady brought them round. Wasn't that nice of her?" Stefanie held my four cards out to me. Neither of them mentioned that I'd forgotten to buy stamps for Anke.

"Let's see," said Stefanie. "Aha, you took four of the youth hostel at twilight. Very nice, really. Are you going to write to your father and mother? And who's going to get the other two?"

"Don't be so **nosy**," Anke snapped at her.

I sat down on her bed and tore one card after another into tiny pieces, until the bed was covered with them. Stefanie wanted to say something, but Anke raised a warning hand. "Leave her," she said softly. "Carlotta needs this just now, for whatever reason."

I fetched the wastepaper basket and slowly and **deliberately** swept all the bits of paper into it. Then I picked up a few that had fallen onto the floor and threw them in as well. Then I put the wastepaper basket back in its place and turned to my mates. "Right, now you can ask me."

"You think writing postcards is stupid and **square**," Anke **conjectured**. "And you wouldn't be wrong there. I don't know what to write to my mother either. I've said 'It's great here,' but, ac-

---

nosy – neugierig; deliberate – bedächtig;
square – spießig;
to conjecture – spekulieren

tually, that isn't true. I've written it extra large so that not very much will fit on the card. Should I go on about the weather? 'Lots of rain, but I've got my waterproof sandals with me.' Or something like that. Is that it, Carlotta? You think it's stupid?"

"No," I countered, "I don't think it's stupid at all. I just don't know who to write to. My mother's somewhere in America, and I don't even know her exact address, and my father would probably prefer to hear from Natascha than from me." I wondered for a moment if I should tell Anke and Stefanie about the thing with the yellow sports car. But perhaps it was better if not too many people knew about that. I had to find a way of helping Jannis out on my own.

"You're imagining things," Stefanie tried to comfort me. "Your father would probably like to hear from both of you."

"Well, **he can wait till the cows come home**," I said quietly. "Because now the card from Natascha is floating down the **sewers** of Erdmannsweiler." And I told them about the card and what I'd done with it.

"I'll help you," said Anke after a moment's thought. We'll **wind** Natascha **up** so much she won't know if she's coming or going. But I don't think she does anyway," she added after a short pause.

He can wait till the cows come home. –
Da kann er lange warten.;
sewers – Kanalisation;
to wind sb. up – jmdn. reizen/ärgern

I smiled. It was good to have a mate. For a moment everything was the way it always used to be between us. But then I remembered Jannis and felt this **gnawing** feeling in my chest. My heart aches, I thought.

Strange, Dad always says he's lost his heart when he's fallen in love. But I'd fallen in love and noticed for the first time where my heart really was. I wondered if Natascha was feeling the same thing. Perhaps her heart ached when she thought of Dad.

"And what shall we do about Jannis?" asked Anke after a while.

Stefanie was drawing little hearts on the card to her family and said nothing. Nor did I. How on earth could I help him? I wondered. And then I had the idea. I would say I'd met Jannis outside this morning at half past five. Bird watching! Then Jannis would have an alibi!

"Hey, Carlotta, couldn't you talk to him again today and I'll watch where you are and come up by chance. You give me a wave and ..." Anke looked at me questioningly.

Stefanie drew a final heart with a **flourish** and followed it with a fat exclamation mark. "I don't think Carlotta should talk to him again," she said slowly. "*I* haven't done anything to help yet. It's my turn now. I'll go and look for Jannis later. Then we'll make our way to the dining room and you come downstairs, Anke, okay?"

Anke shook her head. "No," she said. "Car-

---

gnawing – nagend;
flourish – schwungvolle Bewegung

lotta started and ..." She looked at Stefanie and bit her lower lip in **embarrassment**. "Don't get me wrong, Stefanie, but you're the type every boy falls in love with. And Jannis is very important to me, know what I mean? Don't think that I think you'd ..."

"All right, I get the picture," said Stefanie. "But you don't need to worry on my account. Anyway, Carlotta is just as good-looking."

"But Carlotta is on the job already. I think she should keep at it. Come on, let's go outside and see what the Stuttgart class is doing," Anke suggested. "Perhaps we'll come up with a good idea on the spur of the moment."

The entire hostel seemed **deserted**. "Most of them have gone to the village," the cleaning lady said to us by way of explanation. "And some are with the horses."

"We'll go to the village, too," Anke decided as we were standing uncertainly by the front door. "At least there's something going on there."

"I'm not coming," I said. "Don't be annoyed, but I'd like to be alone for a while."

"And if you see Max, remember what we agreed on!" called Anke as I went upstairs.

I turned around. "Max?" But then I got it. "I'll take care of things."

Our room was in a terrible chaos, but that didn't bother me. The chaos inside me was much worse. I'd probably never get Dad and Natascha

---

embarrassment – Verlegenheit;
deserted – verlassen

apart, and if I did, Dad would certainly **resent** it. And I could give Jannis an alibi, but I wasn't allowed to fall in love with him because Anke had seen him first.

I tore open the window and took a deep breath of fresh air. In the distance, in the field with the horses, I could hear laughter and thought I recognised Heike and Tina. Why were they in such a good **mood**? Angrily, I slammed the window shut and was about to lie down on the bed when the door opened and the cleaning lady appeared behind her **broom**.

"Best go outside while I'm doing in here," she said, pushing me to one side. "Go over to the horses. Girls of your age like them." She reached out for the wastepaper basket **in order to** empty it into the large bin that was standing in the corridor, but she hesitated.

I knew exactly what she was going to say. She had, of course, recognised the scraps of paper.

"I'm off," I said quickly and ran down the corridor. I didn't want to explain why I had torn up four unwritten cards and thrown them away.

On the way to the dining room I **stumbled** into Olli, who was sitting on the floor with his back against the wall listening to music on his Walkman. He had his eyes closed and was **conducting** with his hands. I couldn't help it, I just had to pull

---

to resent – übel nehmen;
mood – Stimmung, Laune;
broom – Besen; in order to – um zu;
to stumble into sb. – *hier:* jmdn. zufällig treffen;
to conduct – dirigieren

out his earphones. He started to **flare up** and be angry, but then he recognised me and grinned from ear to ear.

"Hey, do you have to give a grandad such a fright? I could have had a heart attack."

"*You*," I **mocked**. "If you throw glass vases around the place, you shouldn't be surprised if other people get heart attacks."

He grinned in embarrassment. "It was only supposed to be a little present. My parents always say it's the done thing if you get an invitation. How could I know that the vase was **fragile** and would **make such a racket**? But let's not talk about it. Jessing has laid into me enough already."

I nodded. "Cringe, cringe. What are you listening to? Can I?"

He tried to protest, but I had already got the earphones in and was amazed. Olli had actually been listening to classical music. "What's this, Beethoven?" I guessed.

He nodded. "Beethoven."

"I'd never have thought that of you."

"What then? Folk music?"

"Yes," I laughed. "Folk music. **Clog dancing** and stuff like that."

Olli laughed, too. He seemed to be able to take a joke. "And you? What do you listen to?"

"Oh, all kinds of things. Anything but classi-

---

to flare up – aufbrausen;
to mock – spotten; fragile – zerbrechlich;
to make a racket – Lärm machen;
clog dancing – Schuhplatteln

cal. And above all no opera arias. They drive me mad. Tell me," I hesitated a moment," have you seen Jannis anywhere?"

"I think he wanted to go to the village, at least that's what he said. But if he ran into Jessing, he'll be in the basement **polishing** shoes."

"Polishing shoes? Why?"

"It's one of Jessing's **quirks**. If someone annoys him, they don't get a **detention**, they have to do something for the community. Well, Jannis was the first to run into Jessing at that disastrous birthday party, and Jessing **sentenced** him to polishing shoes. Despite his **injury**."

"Despite his ... injury."

Olli stroked my cheek. "What's up with you? You've gone all white. Can't you stand the sight of blood?"

"No, that's not it," I said. "Of course. Despite his injury."

"Really mean, don't you think? And it was Jannis who cleared up the whole mess. He started to clean up after the stupid vase fell out of my hands and a piece of broken glass got him in the hand. Never seen so much blood. I thought he'd need a doctor."

"Jannis cut himself on a piece of glass!"

Olli looked at me in astonishment. "What's there to laugh about? You're really weird today."

I'd like to have flung my arms around his neck. Jannis had cut himself on a piece of glass. Jannis

---

to polish – *hier:* putzen;
quirk – Macke; detention – Nachsitzen;
to sentence – verurteilen; injury – Verletzung

hadn't jump-started the car, hadn't gone on a **joyride**, wouldn't go to prison. For a short while I was really happy. The thing with Dad and Natascha seemed really far away. I stood up. "Well, I'll be on my way and leave you to your Beethoven."

"By the way, Jannis and I, and maybe a few others from our class, are going jogging at half past five this evening. Would you like to come too? You could bring your two mates, the blonde and the other one," Olli suggested, making a hand gesture that looked as if he was **swishing away** a fly. "Particularly the one with the blond hair."

I turned around, but all I could see was someone disappearing from behind the **frosted glass** of the dining room. Olli grinned at me. "I have just signalled to our teacher that I was in an important meeting and on no account to be disturbed. And because we've **brought him up** to be a good teacher, he disappears. **Prime** example of good teaching methods, don't you think? He also has a guilty conscience because of shouting at me yesterday. Are you coming this evening?"

"Sure!"

Anke would be pleased with me.

---

joyride – Spritztour;
to swish away – wegwischen;
frosted glass – Milchglas;
to bring sb. up – jmdn. erziehen;
prime – erstklassig

Then I strolled

around the hostel for a bit and had a look in the basement, but there was nobody there. The thing about the shoes was probably one of Olli's jokes, I thought. Just before lunch I saw the Stuttgart class collecting lunch packs from the kitchen and getting on a bus.

I sat down in the dining room next to the window and waited for the others. Almost the whole class seemed to have met up in the village. At the head of the small procession coming up the hill I could **make out** Natascha, and beside her Anke and Stefanie. For a moment it gave me a **pang**, but then I remembered what Anke had said that morning and I was relieved again. Anke would have no trouble in **winding up** Dad's new girlfriend, she had no scruples there. I went out onto the terrace and waved to them. As far as I could see from a distance, Natascha didn't look like she'd just been wound up.

"Well?" I greeted my mates as they sat down at my table.

"Great, really great," said Anke with enthusiasm. "Pity you didn't want to come. We discovered a café that even has Internet **access**. Guess

---

to make out – erkennen; pang – Stich;
to wind sb. up – jmdn. ärgern; access – Zugang

what, I found out there's going to be an Internet competition for models. If only I could persuade my mother we needed Internet."

"Actually, I wanted to know how and whether you gave Natascha a wind-up." I couldn't help it, but I sounded pretty annoyed as I said it.

Anke gave me a hurt look. "It's not as easy as you think. First I have to **suss out** the best way to do it."

"While we're on the subject of the best way to do things," I said, "I'd almost forgotten. Jannis is on the jogging **trail** at half past five. Olli asked us if we wanted to come, too."

"Jogging! Are you mad?" Anke looked at me in horror.

"Sorry, it wasn't my idea. Olli suggested it, and I said yes. I thought you absolutely wanted to meet Jannis."

"Yes, sure I want to meet him, but not on the jogging trail. You know I'm useless at sport. There's no way I can go jogging. I'd make a complete and **utter** fool of myself. Jogging, that's the most ..."

"But didn't you tell us once that you won third place in Hamburg ..." I interrupted.

"That was in gymnastics, and anyway, I was younger then and in training."

We finally agreed that I would go to the meeting point and Anke would wait on the field with the horses.

---

to suss out – auskundschaften;
trail – Pfad;
utter – völlig, vollkommen

"I'll go jogging with you. As a support," said Stefanie, smiling at me.

"I hope," Danni said at lunchtime, "that the young ladies have recovered from their nocturnal adventures. Fresh air doesn't seem to be doing some of you much good, so today we won't be going hiking." A storm of applause interrupted him, and he gave an evil grin as he said that the alternative would be a visit to the **local-history** museum in Erdmannsweiler.

"Local-history museum," I could hear Heike grumbling, "on my birthday! This Maths teacher hasn't got a heart."

But she was wrong. After we had trudged through the museum's three rooms, following after Danni, who explained every **farming implement** on the wall, we looked at him in surprise as he stopped in front of a door and suddenly went all mysterious. "We've prepared a little something as a consolation for your unsuccessful party last night. Happy birthday, Heike!" And then he flung the door open.

"Oh, how sweet!" Heike stormed into the farmhouse **parlour**. "How did you know that **crumble** was my favourite cake?"

Danni pointed to Natascha. "She had a **hunch**. Some women have a sixth sense, or whatever, for

---

local-history – Heimatkunde;
farming implement – landwirtschaftliches Gerät;
parlour – Gaststube;
crumble – Streuselkuchen;
hunch – Vorahnung

such things. Sit down everyone. Now for the party."

Natascha sat diagonally opposite me and was in excited conversation with Danni and a woman from the friends of the museum. I couldn't understand anything they were saying because everyone was talking at once. But suddenly the chatter died down, and I could hear quite clearly that Natascha was speaking the Saxon dialect.

"Yes, I come from Saxony," she said, going a little red. "But I only spent my childhood here. When my mother died, my father and I moved to Berlin."

"How old were you then?" asked Danni sympathetically.

"Ten," she said briskly. "And I always longed for a proper family. It isn't very nice to grow up as an only child. But my father had other plans, and it didn't work out." She smiled. "How do you like the cake?"

But our Maths teacher wasn't so easily satisfied. "Natascha isn't your stage name, is it? Excuse me asking so directly, but I don't know much about these things."

"Natascha is my second name. My mother came from Russia and ... well. It was a long time ago."

"But you're still so wonderfully young," said Danni with a fatherly laugh. "You're bound to start a family soon." And he looked the way he always looked when he was handing back a bad piece of work, but trying to reassure the pupil that all hope was not yet lost.

"Did you hear that?" giggled Anke next to me.

"Perhaps he'll ask her to marry him. What do you think? That would be ideal for you. Did you know that Natascha came from Saxony and her mother was Russian?"

I shook my head. What had she just said? It wasn't very nice to grow up as an only child. Actually, I don't know anything at all about Natascha, I thought, and I don't want to know anything about her either. For a moment I was afraid I'd quite like her.

We had to hurry to get back to the youth hostel in time to go jogging. Of course the elastic in my **tracksuit** trousers was still broken, and Stefanie had to help me out with a **safety pin**.

"Just **thread** a new elastic through," she suggested as I was fiddling with the safety pin.

I shrugged. Should I put on a fresh sweatshirt? I stood in front of the cupboard uncertainly and thought about this. But Stefanie was impatient. She probably wanted to prevent me wearing anything nice. I was only supposed to be a go-between after all, and I could do that in any old clothes.

"Don't forget," she reminded me yet again on the way to the jogging trail, "you have to guide Jannis to the horses. By chance Anke is already there, and you have to pretend to be surprised and disappear after three minutes with some kind of excuse, all right?"

---

tracksuit – Jogginganzug;
safety pin – Sicherheitsnadel;
to thread – fädeln

I'd like to have told her to stop playing the great **director**, I knew what I had to do, but instead I said nothing. Stefanie was behaving as if she were friends with me and Anke. But that was only because we were sharing the same room. Things would change once we got home.

We both said nothing. Suddenly Stefanie stood still and looked at me straight in the face. "You're in love with Jannis, too, aren't you?"

At first I wanted to **deny** everything and say something like, "You're crazy, what makes you think such **crap**?" But Stefanie was still looking at me searchingly, and in the end I nodded. "Yes," I said. "It just happened. I didn't want it to. I can't help it. What would you do in my position?"

"I don't know. I'd probably ask myself whose friendship I **valued** most, Anke's or Jannis'. You know Anke much better than him, so ..."

"Thanks," I said. "I don't need any advice. I know what I have to do."

Stefanie wanted to say something, but at that moment Natascha overtook us. She was jogging. For a moment I forgot all my problems. Natascha jogging was a **gift** from above. I couldn't wish for a better hobby for her because Dad hates jogging. He thinks it's idiotic to run through the streets without a proper goal, and he really gets worked up about joggers wearing what Natascha was wearing: colourful tracksuit, sweatband and trainers of a particular **brand**.

---

director – Regisseur/-in;
to deny – leugnen; crap – Unsinn;
to value – wertschätzen; gift – Geschenk; brand – Marke

I decided to send him a postcard that evening, telling him that I'd come across his new girlfriend in full jogging gear, and what about that as a nice new hobby?

We reached the jogging **circuit** at half past five **on the dot**.

I saw Jannis immediately. He had a thick bandage around his right hand. Olli and the other boy from his class were standing next to the hut, laughing softly.

Olli said a mumbled hello when he saw us. The other boy gave an embarrassed grin, and Jannis said nothing. He was bending down to fasten his trainers tighter. Then he stood up straight, but didn't look at me. Stefanie didn't say anything either. A nice evening *this* was going to be.

"I think it's going to rain," said Olli, looking rather worried. "Do you think we should go into the hut?"

Rain! Olli had to be mad. For the first time we were in Erdmannsweiler the sky was perfectly clear. There wasn't a cloud to be seen for miles.

Jannis tapped his forehead and murmured, "You're crazy."

Then we were silent again. Stefanie finally suggested we make a start, but Olli shook his head. "Let's wait a bit longer."

Wait? What did Olli want to wait for? I wanted to ask him, but then I saw Natascha in the distance, coming towards us in her **wacky** tracksuit. She would soon be here.

---

circuit – Rundweg; on the dot – auf die Sekunde genau; wacky – exzentrisch

Olli **screwed up** his eyes and **surveyed** the trail. Then he looked at his watch. Jannis was fiddling with his shoelaces again.

Natascha was at shouting distance, and I expected to hear something encouraging from her like, "What are you all doing here? Do you want to come for a run?" But she said nothing. She jogged past us and didn't even wave. We watched her until she disappeared into some trees.

"Hey, didn't your mate want to come, too? The one with the blond hair?" asked Olli. "Not that it's particularly important, I'm just interested."

I looked at Stefanie. "Go! Now's your chance," said her eyes. I cleared my throat and avoided looking at Jannis. "Anke didn't want to come with us. She likes horses so much. We're going to jog for a bit and then meet her in the field. You can come with us if you like."

It sounded terribly calculated to me, and then I remembered the lie I'd told about Jannis' horse allergy and hoped Stefanie had forgotten it.

"Yeah, why not?" said Olli. "What do you think, Jannis? And you, Christoph?" The two of them nodded and trotted off with Stefanie.

Suddenly the ice was broken. I heard Jannis laughing when Stefanie took a run at a tree and tried to climb it while Christoph and Olli did a funny dance on a tree trunk. I ran on mechanically until – for the second time that day – I almost stumbled over Olli.

---

to screw up – zusammenkneifen;
to survey – überblicken

He was sitting on the ground rubbing his knee. "Old age," he grinned when he saw me looking at him. "I've done my **lap of honour**. I'm a year older than the others, and it shows." He stood up and **limped** a couple of **paces**. "And apart from that I hate jogging."

"So why are you here?"

He sighed. "This was my mate Jannis' brilliant idea. That blonde friend of yours, what's her name again?"

"Anke."

"Ah yes. What's she like?"

To Jannis, I should have **enthused about** Anke at this point, which was what I'd promised her. But not a word had been said about Olli. I shrugged my shoulders. "Oh, she's quite nice."

He probably noticed I didn't want to talk about her and told me a funny story about his Maths teacher, who had hidden behind a newspaper during a test. "Guess what, he had cut two eye-holes in it, and we thought he was watching us. Until someone went up to the front to ask him something and noticed he had shut his eyes and gone to sleep."

Jannis, Stefanie and Christoph were already waiting for us at the hut. "Here comes our marathon winner," roared Christoph. "Olli, the fastest **snail** of all time, crawls into the stadium. **Deafening** applause from the stands ..."

---

lap of honour – Ehrenrunde; to limp – hinken; pace – Schritt; to enthuse about sb. – in Begeisterung über jmdn. ausbrechen; snail – Schnecke; deafening – ohrenbetäubend

"Can't you shut up for one minute?" Jannis snapped at him. He looked questioningly at Olli, and suddenly I thought I knew what was going on. Of course, how could I have been so stupid? I could have laughed, but it would probably have sounded heartless. Jannis wanted to get to know Anke the whole time, and Olli was supposed to arrange it through me. Which was why he had asked about her so often. Which was why he had suggested going jogging. And I, like a fool, had hoped for a moment that Jannis was interested in *me*. As if! He had never even looked at me.

Christoph had had enough. "You can go to the horses on your own. I'm going back to the hostel," he announced. "There's so little food here I want to get a good starting position. An advantage over the others. The snails, so to speak," he added with a grin.

"I'm not coming either," said Stefanie.

"Not enough food here for you either?" inquired Christoph.

She laughed. "No, it's not that. But I always sneeze around horses. I probably have a horse allergy."

"Is there such a thing?" asked Jannis. "I've only heard of an allergy to cats."

I'd have liked the ground to swallow me up. Stefanie turned to me. "But didn't you say that ..."

"I think we should get a move on," I interrupted her. "Shall we go on over to the field?"

Stefanie gave me an unfriendly look and murmured, "You never let people finish their sentences, do you?" But then she trotted back to the youth hostel behind Christoph. I breathed a sigh of relief.

I strolled over to the horses with Jannis and Olli. I had the ridiculous hope that Anke wouldn't be there for some reason or other. Perhaps she'd been discovered as the model of the future by some star photographer from Hamburg or New York.

But I could see her standing next to the horses from a long way away. She had dressed herself up to match the **rural** surroundings: jeans, red-and-white checked blouse and a grey flannel jacket. The jacket seemed familiar. Of course, she must have borrowed it from Natascha. Perhaps that was how Anke wanted to wind her up, the way she'd promised.

I'll never forget the sight: Anke with her long, golden blond hair, in the mild evening sunlight, feeding grass to the horses. No wonder Jannis had fallen in love with her. I involuntarily looked down at myself. I was all sweaty, and the safety pin on the waistband of my tracksuit trousers was clearly visible. Now I'd really have liked to **vanish into thin air**.

"Oh," said Anke, looking rather surprised. "Were you going jogging?"

"No, what makes you think that?" asked Olli.

"But ..." Anke began, before it clicked. "You're quite a joker." She looked discretely at her watch.

---

rural – ländlich, Land-;
to vanish into thin air – sich in Luft auflösen

I understood.

Olli also seemed to be in a hurry suddenly. "I think I'll go on over before Christoph eats up all our supper. He has no scruples when it comes to food. What about you, Anke, would you like to come, too? I bought a great CD in Dresden. I could lend it to you."

I couldn't believe my ears. Olli, funny little Olli, was also keen on Anke. **Pensively**, she stroked one of the horses' **manes** and smiled at Jannis from the side. He didn't **turn a hair**. Of course, he wanted to talk to Anke once Olli and I had disappeared.

"I'll go, too," I said. "The jogging has done me in."

Anke would be satisfied with me. I had delivered her Jannis and **made myself scarce** after three minutes.

Jannis and Olli stared at me. Anke laughed. "Our Carlotta isn't much of a sportswoman."

"Just a minute ..." called Olli, but I didn't hear the end of the sentence. I had turned round abruptly and run off.

"Our Carlotta isn't much of a sportswoman!" I heard Anke's words over and over again. To my mind, they sounded mocking. Anke, who didn't want to go jogging because she was out of breath after five metres, who was always inventing new excuses in sports so as not to have to take part. Anke, who I'd done so much for.

---

pensive – nachdenklich; mane – Mähne;
to turn a hair – sich rühren;
to make oneself scarce – sich rar machen

Blind with tears I ran straight into the arms of Mr Dannitzki, who was sitting in front of the youth hostel in the evening sunshine. "What's wrong with you?" he asked, startled.

"Horse-hair allergy," I stammered. I couldn't think of anything better just at that moment. "It always affects my eyes."

"Allergies are becoming more and more common," began Danni. "It's because of our unhealthy lifestyle. Fifty years ago, for example ..."

At that moment Tina came out of the hostel, and I fled. Thankfully, I didn't meet anyone on the way to our room. Without changing I lay down on my bed and thought a million evil thoughts. Anke! I'd probably never talk to her again. Jannis! Hopefully he hadn't noticed how much I liked him. The worst was the thought of seeing the two of them together, holding hands probably. I wouldn't be able to bear it. My only hope was the hike Mr Dannitzki had threatened.

"If the weather's more or less on our side, we'll explore the surrounding countryside again on our last day. We won't be able to make our trip to Dresden, but there's a thing or two to discover around here," he had said at breakfast, and most of us had grumbled quite a bit. Me too. But now I would have walked a hundred kilometres in the pouring rain so as not to have to put up with the sight of new young love.

I heard footsteps in the corridor. Someone came into the room.

"Carlotta, is everything all right?" I heard Stefanie whispering. "Tina said you had an allergy. But it isn't true, is it?"

I shook my head. I couldn't say a word, otherwise I'd have cried.

Stefanie climbed up onto my bed. "It's because of Jannis, isn't it?" She looked at me **at a loss**. "My mother always says that if ever I'm **lovesick,** I shouldn't see it too absolutely. It'll pass. Time **heals** all wounds."

"Adults don't understand," I said in a **muffled** voice.

Stefanie slid a packet of **paper tissues** out of her trouser pocket and put them on my pillow. I tried to smile.

"By the way, have you heard the latest? Carlotta, I have to tell you an incredible story. I've just heard it in the dining room. Do you know who wrecked the yellow sports car? It was the warden's brother. The one who picked you up from the station. Do you remember him? His sister had never lent him the car, so he just broke in, jump-started it and was off. And then after about 200 metres he drove it into a ditch."

I smiled. "Amazing story."

Stefanie looked at me searchingly. "Would you like some of my dessert?" she asked. "There was tiramisu, and I brought it up specially for you. You should eat something."

"Yes," I said, knowing for sure that I wouldn't be able to eat a thing for the next few days.

"I'm going back to the dining room. Danni's

---

at a loss – verlegen;
to be lovesick – Liebeskummer haben;
to heal – heilen; muffled – *hier:* erstickt;
paper tissue – Papiertaschentuch

doing a quiz and ... Don't you want to come, too? Some **distraction** might do you good."

"I have to get through this alone," I said. "Thanks. Thanks for the tiramisu."

The next morning I woke up really early because the sun was shining directly onto my face. I turned over onto my side and my gaze fell on the many **scrunched-up** paper tissues next to my pillow, and straight away I remembered Jannis and Anke. Because the weather was so good for hiking I'd hardly see them, I hoped. Perhaps we ought to try and convince Danni to take us on a night hike right after the day one. Then there wouldn't be an evening meal with the Stuttgarters.

Relieved, I went back to sleep.

Someone was throwing open the window when I woke up. Rain was drumming on the garage roof in front of our room.

"Country rain," announced Stefanie with satisfaction. "Not even Danni will go out in this weather. Our hike will be well and truly off."

I knew it. I always had bad luck. But I would be a good loser. At least **outwardly**.

I looked down **warily**. There was no sign of Anke.

Stefanie noticed what I was doing. "She got up first for a change. I think she's already at breakfast."

---

distraction – Ablenkung; scrunched-up – zerknüllt; outwardly – äußerlich; wary – vorsichtig

I could imagine why Anke, the **late-riser**, was already downstairs. She was probably sitting in the dining room next to her Jannis, and I'd have to go past the two of them and try to look normal.

I'd like to have stayed in bed, but I was hungry. The bowl of tiramisu was still standing by my pillow, but with all the will in the world I had no stomach for it.

"It was really fun yesterday evening," said Stefanie. "First the quiz, which wasn't so great. I had to compete against Tina in the final, and even Albert Einstein wouldn't have stood a chance against her. But then Natascha taught me and Danni a new card game. You should have seen us. Danni kept trying to increase his chances through logic." She laughed. "He said you had to have a plan, but Natascha and I just played by intuition. And guess who always lost."

I shrugged. I wasn't in the least bit interested.

"Just think, Danni lost. He shouldn't have made a plan, but just played from the heart. That's what Natascha said. I quite like her, actually."

"How nice for you," I muttered, pulling on a fresh sweatshirt.

Stefanie looked at me in astonishment. "Isn't it over yet?"

I shook my head. She didn't have a clue. But what could you expect from someone who had fallen in love with two white mice. "No, but I don't want to talk about it."

Stefanie thought for a moment. She wanted to

---

late-riser – Spätaufsteher/-in

comfort me, that was clear. "I'll teach you the card game tomorrow on the way home," she said. "Oh yes, and the best thing about yesterday evening was that Danni made a mistake when he added up the points. And he's a Maths teacher. Isn't that amazing?"

I nodded and said I thought it was really amazing and decided to have a shower first and wash my hair. I didn't want to look like **misery** in person when I entered the dining room.

At around half past eight I felt capable of going down to breakfast. I would wave at Anke and Jannis and then sit somewhere with my back to them.

I took some deep breaths before I opened the dining-room door. I'd never tell anyone that under the shower I'd murmured to myself, "I'm strong, I'm beautiful, I'll come through." Perhaps self-hypnosis would work better for me than for Anke.

But I could have saved the effort.

A quick look around showed me that only a few places in the dining room were taken. Anke was sitting next to Danni and talking to Natascha. There was nothing to be seen of Jannis and his class, which was reassuring, more or less. Anke waved to me, but I ignored her and sat next to Andrea, who looked at me with curiosity.

"I heard you had a horse allergy yesterday and were all swollen up," she mumbled with her mouth full. "It still shows. You look a bit weird."

---

misery – Elend

"Thanks," I said. "Lovely way to say hello." I stood up and sat down at an empty table.

But of course I didn't even have two minutes' peace and quiet, because there was Natascha standing in front of me playing the worried **surrogate** mother. "Aren't you feeling well? You're so pale," she said, sitting down. "Would you like to talk about things?"

I turned my head to the window in refusal. The rain had stopped, and behind Erdmannsweiler you could even see a bit of blue sky. With any luck the hike would take place after all.

"Carlotta, please!" I could see quite clearly she'd like to have given a melodramatic sigh. But because it suddenly went quiet around us, she didn't **have the bottle**. "I have to give you something afterwards, but it's upstairs. This morning as I ..."

I looked her straight in the face. "Natascha, I don't want anything from you. I'm not interested in this morning. I just want to be left alone."

Bull's eye! Let her run to the telephone and complain to Dad. I didn't care. The thing I was really interested in was what was going on between Anke and Jannis. Anke didn't look particularly happy the way she was sitting next to Danni, staring at her plate. But she was probably just waiting for it to be evening when the Stuttgarters would come back from their hike and she would have her Jannis again.

Natascha had stood up without a word and

---

surrogate – Ersatz-;
to have the bottle – Mumm haben

gone over to the door, where she almost bumped into Stefanie.

"Everyone's in a wonderful mood today," she said as she sat down at my table. "Have you any idea what's up with Natascha? I think she was crying."

"No," I said, I didn't have a clue and I didn't care either.

"And have you also heard that the Stuttgarters left this morning at half past six? I found out just now at reception. The warden was pretty annoyed about the catastrophic state of some of their rooms and ..."

"They left? This morning?" I interrupted. "But Olli said that ..."

"Olli!" My friend laughed out loud. "Olli doesn't know a thing. And anyway, he mumbles so much you can never understand what he's saying."

"You're quite sure they've gone?" I asked again. That, of course, explained Anke's bad mood. "You're quite sure?" I could have hugged Stefanie. Perhaps I was going to be in luck for once in my life. Outside there was a moderate shower of rain, but I was **radiant**. "A short happiness in love for Anke," said an evil little voice in my head.

"Perhaps we should see to Anke for a moment," I suggested.

Stefanie was pleased and nodded. "It would be great if you'd make things up with her. I feel

---

radiant – strahlend

so stupid when you two are angry with one another. I want to be fair, but I don't know who ..."

"It's all right," I said, chewing my breakfast. "Don't worry. I'll go over to Anke."

"Hey, what was that about your allergy?" Anke wanted to know as I sat down beside her. "Everyone was so worried about you, and when I came into the room yesterday to wake you up, Stefanie snapped at me and said I should let you sleep and you weren't feeling at all well."

She pointed a finger at my left eye. "You still look all puffed up. I didn't know you had an allergy."

"I didn't know either," I said. "But I feel better now. And what about you?"

She laughed **sullenly**. "Hey, guess what, Danni just told me I was going to get an E for my Maths oral. He asked me if I had something against him, because I always talked to the people sitting next to me but never to him. He thought he was being funny. Typical Maths-teacher humour. At any rate, I have to do better than a D in the next test, otherwise ... On the other hand, once I've got my contract as a model, I definitely won't need to know how to do Maths any more." She sighed softly. "Do you think I should dye my hair a darker shade? I think blond is mega out."

"Could be," I murmured. Why wasn't she saying a word about Jannis? "And yesterday

---

sullen – düster

evening?" I tried to make the question sound pretty uninterested, but I couldn't avoid the light **quake** in my voice. "How was yesterday evening?"

"A fantastic quiz, in which our Tina was the glorious winner, of course. Danni asked life's essential questions." She laughed when she saw my astonished face. "Well, you had to know, for example, how long a ten-euro note was. Or the name of Alexander the Great's wife. And idiotic stuff like that."

"And what is her name?"

Anke shrugged. "I don't know any more. I don't weigh myself down with garbage like that. Or do you think an agency will take me just because I can say her name backwards and forwards?" She roared with laughter. "In that case Tina would be the next Claudia Schiffer."

Anke had taken part in the quiz, so she couldn't have met up with Jannis again after supper, I thought. But perhaps the Stuttgarters took part too and ..."

"And what about Jannis?" It just burst out of me. I hadn't wanted to ask so directly, but I just couldn't help it.

"Oh yes, Jannis," said Anke, pretending to find it difficult to remember who he was. She grinned in embarrassment. "You know what, I don't think he's right for me after all. We stood around in the field for a while, but he hardly said a word. I had to drag everything out of him.

---

quake – Zittern

Dreadful." She pulled a face. "After a while I couldn't think of anything else to say and asked him about his horse allergy. But he just looked at me and said he didn't know about that and he wasn't allergic to anything. I felt like a right **wally**, you can imagine."

I nodded. How had I come up with such rubbish?

"At least when I said I had this information from you, he **perked up** a bit. He wanted to know why you'd left so suddenly. For a moment I even thought he was in love with you. Anyway, he wanted to know quite a few things about you, but I was fed up with standing around in a **damp** field – I only had sandals on after all – and I told him if he wanted to see you, he only had to wait outside the dining room after supper. And that's what he did, but you didn't turn up."

"Jannis waited for me?" I asked **tonelessly**.

"Yes, until the stupid quiz started. Then the Stuttgarters' teacher called them all in, and they had to compete with us. It wasn't fair, of course, because we had Tina. They had no chance against her."

"And are you frustrated because Jannis isn't in love with you?" I asked cautiously.

Anke thought for a moment. "You know, I told him about my plan to become a model, but he just wasn't interested. I don't think that's a good basis for a relationship. I need a boyfriend who's

---

wally – Trottel;
to perk up – aufheitern; damp – feucht;
toneless – tonlos

totally behind the idea. Someone who'll come to New York or wherever, and who understands a thing or two about the business. And about advertising contracts and whatever else it all **involves**. It just didn't click with Jannis." She laughed. "As my aunt always says, 'You can lead a horse to water, but you can't make him drink.' And **in regard to** men I think she's dead right."

I could have flung my arms about her neck. Anke wasn't interested in Jannis any more, and instead Jannis seemed to be interested in *me*. Life was simply wonderful.

"Breakfast seems to have done you good," said my mate. "You look much better."

But I was only better for a minute or so. Then I remembered that the Stuttgarters had left that morning. I would never see him again.

"But at least," said Anke, gathering up her cup and plate, "Jannis made Erdmannsweiler a bit more interesting. Berlin would have been better, but what the hell."

---

to involve – *hier:* umfassen, einschließen;
in regard to – was betrifft

If I hadn't

gone to bed yesterday ... If I'd gone to supper like a normal person ... If I hadn't just **cracked up** right away ... I had done everything wrong yet again, I thought, as I ran after Anke and Stefanie along the narrow path through the wood. Danni, at the front of our procession, was in a hurry. The next **downpour** was **due** in half an hour at the latest, and before that he wanted to show us what he'd been looking for all this time.

"Probably blue **daisies**," said Anke mockingly, turning round to me, "or perhaps a **four-leafed clover**. Are you feeling better?"

I tried to smile. "I feel brilliant. I really come to life when Danni **dashes** us through the bush," I said, and Anke laughed.

In the dining room I had asked her **in passing** about Jannis's school in Stuttgart, but she didn't have a clue. Perhaps I could find out something at reception, I hoped. I hung around there for a

---

to crack up – zusammenbrechen;
downpour – Regenguss; to be due – fällig sein;
daisy – Gänseblümchen;
four-leafed clover – vierblättriges Kleeblatt;
to dash – *hier:* treiben; in passing – nebenbei

while, intensely studying a notice saying that a gold chain had been found in the bakery and reading the train timetable three times until I almost knew it by heart. When there was no one else around apart from me, the warden asked, "And what do you want?"

I had thought very clearly about what I wanted to say. "One of the boys from Stuttgart, the ones who left this morning, lent me his Walkman," I lied. "And of course I have to give it back. It's so embarrassing, know what I mean?"

The woman nodded. "And why are you telling me this?"

"Well, perhaps you could give me the address of the school. Then I could send the Walkman back and ..."

The warden thought for a moment. "The papers are in the office. Come back in half an hour and I'll give you the address. Or do you want the address of the teacher?"

"No, no. The name and address of the school will do," I said and felt pleased with myself. I didn't quite know what my next step would be, but a little plan was already forming in my mind.

Once I knew the address of Jannis's school, I might be able to suggest to Dad that we make a trip to Stuttgart. The magic word would be 'Staatsgalerie'. If I showed an interest in art, Dad would definitely be prepared to **excuse** me from school. I knew him all too well. Then we'd have a look around and just by chance walk past Jan-

---

to excuse – entschuldigen

nis' school, ideally around one o'clock. I'd need a bit of luck, but why shouldn't I get lucky for once?

Half an hour later I was back at reception. At first the woman didn't know what I wanted any more, but then she laughed. "Those boys, dreadful. You can't imagine the stuff they left behind. And the teacher was the same. He left his compass under the bed. Well, I hope they find their way back home." She thought for a moment. "Why don't you just bring me the Walkman? We don't want you to forget it as well."

It was pointless. The warden wanted to make up a big parcel and send everything on that Jannis's class had forgotten: the compass, a pair of pyjamas, three toothbrushes, two **odd** socks, a broken umbrella, two baseball caps and this Walkman. When I cautiously suggested sending the Walkman myself, she got all annoyed. "Does that mean you don't trust me?" she asked angrily.

"No, of course not," I assured her.

Just at that moment Mr Dannitzki came downstairs and saw me. "Carlotta, **chop chop**, we want to get going," he called.

"Just a moment," said the warden and told him the whole story.

Danni **glared at** me. "I don't understand why you don't want to send the Walkman with the other things. You can wrap it in **polystyrene**,

---

odd – *hier:* ungleich; cop chop – dalli, dalli;
to glare at sb. – jmdn. zornig anstarren;
polystyrene – Styropor

then it definitely won't get broken. You should be thankful someone's saving you the bother. Go on, what are you waiting for? Go up and fetch the Walkman so we can finally be off."

"Yes," I said. I couldn't think of anything else. From my room I fetched the Walkman Jenny had given me for my last birthday and handed it to the warden without a word. I didn't dare say I'd already given back the borrowed one and only forgotten doing so. And anyway, I didn't care any more.

I just had to forget Jannis, I thought, trudging behind the class through the muddy wood.

"Danni says only five more minutes. The way he always miscalculates, that certainly means another hour," Anke bitched.

But just for a change our Maths teacher was right. After exactly five minutes we turned aside from the path, crawled through thick **undergrowth** – Anke in sandals! – and came out into a small **clearing**. Mr Dannitzki made a **solemn** face. He was standing next to a large stone in the middle and touching it carefully with his hand.

"We're in a magic **hollow**," he said in a low voice. Some of us giggled. Since when had our Maths teacher believed in magic? "According to legend, this is a wishing stone. Many, many years ago a young man wanted to marry a girl

---

undergrowth – Gestrüpp;
clearing – Lichtung;
solemn – feierlich;
hollow – Senke

from the village, but he didn't have any money. One night he sat down on this stone and decided to leave the country. Then along came a good **fairy** and …"

"... they all lived happily ever after," I heard someone saying softly behind me. "I didn't know our Danni was such a romantic."

"The youth of today," said our Maths teacher to Natascha in resignation. You don't have to believe in it, but I think this clearing has something magical about it."

"He's right," whispered Stefanie to me. "Look at the grey sky and the fields. If I was here alone, I'd find it really **creepy**."

"And what do you have to do exactly for the wish to come true?" asked Natascha. She seemed really serious, as if she believed in it.

"Touch the stone, nothing else. But you must not have any bad thoughts in you, otherwise it doesn't work. Or rather, luckily it doesn't work. So you can only wish for good things," Danni explained. He took Natascha's hand and placed it on the stone. "Don't you want to make a wish?"

For a moment it looked as if she wanted to take her hand away quickly. But then she said, "Yes, I do want to make a wish."

I had the impression she was looking in my direction. I'd like to have wished that Natascha's wish wouldn't come true, but that didn't work of course. So I pretended I was admiring the view.

Anke came and stood next to me and smirked.

---

fairy – Fee;
creepy – gruselig

"I put my hand on the stone and wished for a D in my Maths oral. Danni was standing right next to me. He must have heard. Now I hope the magic works, too. He *has* to give me a D at last, don't you think? Otherwise he'd be admitting it was just a normal stone."

I nodded and assured her it was very clever of her.

Anke was a bit annoyed she hadn't asked for a C or even a B.

She was about to put her hand on the stone again when Danni called out, "Be careful. It only works once. A second wish automatically cancels out the first one." He grinned. "Anke, I can only warn you. You could easily end up with an even worse mark." He looked up at the sky. "According to my calculations the next shower will be on us in a quarter of an hour. If we hurry, we won't get too wet. So come along, ladies."

Inconspicuously I stretched out my hand to the stone. I wished as hard as I could to see Jannis again some time. The thought of him was so powerful it almost hurt.

"Carlotta, come *on*," I heard Stefanie calling. I stroked the stone again, said Jannis, Jannis, Jannis quietly three times and crawled through the undergrowth to the others.

Of course I knew it was all humbug. There was no way a stone could **fulfil** wishes. And anyway, you couldn't have any bad thoughts while you were wishing, but those were exactly what I'd

---

to fulfil – erfüllen

had. Natascha's wish shouldn't come true. She shouldn't get Dad, I'd thought, which meant the end of my Jannis wish. Oh well, I thought, at least I tried.

"And remember, everything has to be packed by tomorrow morning," Natascha called out after the evening meal. "Our train's leaving at 7:19 and . . ." She looked at Danni. "When do we have to be at the station? Ten past seven?"

Danni smiled **grimly**. "With this chaotic class? Seven on the dot and not a second later."

"But why so early?" moaned Anke next to me. "We'll just stand around in the station, and the train will probably be late anyway."

Everyone **grouched**; even Tina and Agnes mumbled something to themselves. Natascha had bent down to Danni and was talking to him quietly.

"Just as an exception, ladies, I'm prepared to go against one of my hard-and-fast rules. And only thanks to Ms Lewin here. She says it would really be too hard on you to stand around on the platform for so long. So all right, 7:10, but that's my last word. And if we miss the train because of some **blockhead** . . ."

The rest was lost in a general murmur.

"I think 7:10 is still pretty early," I heard Stefanie saying next to me. "Carlotta, what's wrong with you? You're looking **peculiar**."

---

grim – grimmig;
to grouch – nörgeln; blockhead – Dummkopf;
peculiar – eigenartig

"Nothing's wrong," I replied. Natascha had said that the train left at 7:19. That couldn't be right, I was certain. Natascha was probably about to score the biggest own goal of her life.

Just to be on the safe side I went to reception after supper, and a quick look was enough to convince me. Of course I'd been right. The train at 7:19 only went on Sundays and public holidays. Our train, on the other hand, left at 7:05 and we wouldn't even be able to wave it goodbye.

I could have cheered. Because of Natascha we'd miss our train. Danni would go ballistic. Natascha might as well give up. How stupid can you get, not to be able to read a timetable properly!

I had to tell Anke about it really quickly. On the stairs I met Natascha. The few days in the hostel had left their mark on her, and she looked tired and stressed out. Perhaps she wasn't properly made up either. Tomorrow morning at 7:19 she would look even older.

I wanted to be pleased about this, actually, but it didn't work. I'm so mean, I thought. It isn't fair to drop Natascha in it like this. She hadn't really done anything against me, if you didn't count being Dad's new girlfriend.

"By the way, the departure time isn't right," I heard myself saying. "If I were you, I'd have a look at the timetable in reception."

She wanted to say something, but I turned around and ran up the stairs. What happened next, wasn't my worry. Natascha had made her bed, now she had to lie in it.

"Was Natascha bothering you again?" asked Anke, who was standing at the top of the stairs. "She really knows how to get on people's nerves."

"She wanted to know what time it was," I said. "Come on, let's go and see what the others are doing."

A short while later Danni **rounded** us **up** again. He and Ms Lewin had decided that an earlier train was more **convenient**; we'd get home sooner, he explained. And he was dead right because the 7:19 train didn't leave until next Sunday.

A few of us protested that it didn't matter if we got home earlier or later, but Danni was **unrelenting**. "Ten to seven at the station. That's my final word."

Natascha was standing next to him looking rather pale. On her way out she said softly to me, "Thanks for the tip. Without you everything would have gone wrong. I want to ..."

I shook my head. "I haven't got time." She shouldn't think things were going to be different from now on.

We finished packing just before eleven. Stefanie crawled under the beds and **re-emerged** covered in **fluff** to tell us "I couldn't find anything except **dustballs**."

---

to round up – zusammentrommeln;
convenient – geeignet;
unrelenting – unerbittlich;
to re-emerge – wieder auftauchen;
fluff – Fluse; dustballs – Staubflocken

"Come on, let's **take** Danni **for a bit of a ride**," Anke suggested. She took a sheet of paper and wrote on it in red felt pen: *Your incredibly interesting. Your my dream man*. She screwed it up and threw it under Stefanie's bed.

"Are you crazy?" shouted Stefanie. "You made at least three spelling mistakes. And if Danni finds it and then finds out it was my bed, then ..."

"Then he'll think you find him interesting and he's your dream man," laughed Anke. "Nice thought, isn't it?"

Stefanie crawled under the bed for the second time that evening. "Ugh," she cried out in horror. "There must be a spider under here. What I thought were dustballs are **cobwebs**. Anke, what direction did you chuck that paper in? Hey, what's going on? Why have you put the light out?"

We didn't have anything to do with it. Neither Anke nor I had been anywhere near the light switch. "It's probably a **short circuit**," Anke guessed. "I'll look for a torch."

There was an ear-splitting scream from the corridor. I tore open the door and saw a figure dressed in white with **bloodshot** eyes dancing up and down in front of Tina's room. "I am Abdul the Terrible," it howled, "and I want Tina this very night."

---

to take sb. for a ride – jmdn. auf die Schippe nehmen;
cobweb – Spinnwebe;
short circuit – Kurzschluss;
bloodshot – blutunterlaufen

The ghost was rattling on the door, but in vain. Tina probably locked her room at night as a **pre-caution**.

"What is this **hellish** noise?" Danni came round the corner with a torch in his hand and had to suppress a grin. "Aha, the hostel ghost in person." He seized the figure by the ear and dragged it away.

"Ouch, you're hurting me," Heike complained, trying to break free.

But Danni was stronger. "Oh no, you don't," he said. "I actually thought that girls of your age had grown out of such idiotic ideas as scaring their classmates. But I probably **overestimated** you. And while you're still awake, Heike, you can go and **screw** the **fuses** back in and then you can **sweep** all the rooms. And no arguments."

"But the others were involved, too," Heike protested.

She could have saved her breath. All the doors – which had been wide open up to a few seconds ago because no one wanted to miss anything – suddenly closed.

"There's absolutely no one here apart from you," we heard Danni saying.

A little while later the light came back on. Armed with a broom, Heike knocked on all the

---

precaution – Vorsichtsmaßnahme;
hellish – höllisch;
to overestimate – überschätzen;
to screw – drehen, schrauben;
fuse – Sicherung;
to sweep – kehren, fegen

doors and swept all the rooms under Danni's supervision. Natascha had suggested doing it the next morning, but Danni was unmoved. "Never put off till tomorrow what you can do today."

Heike finished at around midnight. Only Tina and Andrea refused to open their door, even though our Maths teacher assured them three times that it was all harmless and no one was playing tricks on them.

"If Heike hadn't made such a racket, Danni wouldn't have realised what was going on," said Anke with a yawn. "Anyway, I've had enough of youth hostels and stuff for a while. I'll be glad to be back home, I can tell you. I think I'll have my hair cut short. It looks more sporty, don't you think?"

Stefanie mumbled something inaudible into her pillow and said nothing. I wanted to stay awake the whole night thinking of Jannis. It's the last time, I told myself. At home I have other problems and I can't burden myself with **unrequited** love. It'll take up all my energy, which I need to get Dad and his new girlfriend apart. Still thinking of Jannis, I saw from the **luminous dial** of my wristwatch that it was half past one. Then I fell asleep.

At ten to seven we were standing, totally exhausted, in Erdmannsweiler's little railway station, counting our classmates, our luggage and the minutes till the train's departure.

---

unrequited – unerwidert;
luminous dial – Leuchtzifferblatt

"I don't understand why Danni forced us to be here so early. I think it's pure **harassment**," said Anke rather loudly as our Maths teacher came past on his second count (he'd probably miscounted the first time).

Danni hesitated, then grinned. "What's that you're saying, Anke? By the way, I wanted to talk to you about your spelling. I found a note from you this morning. Tut, tut!" He shook his head thoughtfully. "Haven't you learnt that 'interesting' is written with one r? It comes from the Latin *inter esse* and means ..."

Anke had fled behind the **pile** of luggage. She was trying to smile, but you could see she was pretty embarrassed.

"I thought the note had disappeared," I said to Stefanie.

She shook her head. "It turned up again when Heike swept our room." She bent over to me. "And I kicked it under Anke's bed because I was so annoyed with her – I thought the note was totally childish – and that's where Danni found it this morning when he checked the rooms."

"So now, of course, he thinks it came from Anke."

"And he's right, isn't he?"

Our train came in at exactly 7:05. Anke and I were about to go and look for a compartment to ourselves when the voice of our Maths teacher rang out. "One moment, ladies. Carlotta Bergmann and Anke Bauder are under my personal

---

harassment – Schikane;
pile – Stapel

protection. They may only leave their **designated** compartment with my expressed permission," he announced to **raucous** laughter from the whole class. "Otherwise we'll lose them again."

"I wonder who'll pick me up from the station," thought Stefanie out loud. "My father works till half past six, but my mother will definitely come. And I'm looking forward to seeing my mice. Max and Moritz, I've told you about them." She laughed happily. "Actually, I'm really looking forward to being back home."

Anke pulled a face. "Well, I don't know. We've got school again next week. I mustn't think about it." She stretched her **limbs**. "When I have my contract as a model, I'll invite you to Berlin. Or perhaps I'll be living in New York. Then you'll see there's a life outside of school, too."

I was about to say, "If only there were no whens and ifs," when I heard the guard reading out the connecting trains over the loudspeaker. "ICE to Stuttgart ..." I closed my eyes for a moment. For the whole of my life I'd probably only think of Jannis when I heard Stuttgart.

Then I remembered that I didn't want to think about him any more because I had to solve a completely different problem. But perhaps things didn't look too bad. Natascha was actually running through the train in her pink tracksuit. She probably even thought it looked chic and

---

designated – zugewiesen;
raucous – lauthals;
limb – Gliedmaße

was the right kind of thing to wear for a journey. I assumed she wouldn't change before we arrived, and that was my hope.

"I have to phone my father and tell him to meet me at the station," I said to Anke and Stefanie. "Do you think I should report to Danni?"

They both giggled, and I crept past Danni's compartment. He wouldn't have noticed anyway because he had fallen asleep with his hiking maps on his knees. The last few days had probably stressed him out quite a lot. He was over 50 after all – almost a pensioner, as Anke had mockingly said. Natascha's pink tracksuit shone out at me from the end of the corridor. She was standing at the window talking to Andrea and Heike.

"Carlotta, wait a moment," she called when she saw me. "I'd like to ..."

I shook my head. "Sorry, I'm in a hurry. I want to call my father."

I just had to rub her nose in it. Although, of course, she had no idea that the call would bring her closer to the end of her relationship with Dad. I successfully fought back the **teeny-weeny** trace of a guilty conscience. I'll let fate decide, I said to myself. If Dad doesn't answer by the third ring, I'll hang up. But if he does, it'll be a sign from heaven.

He answered on the third ring.

"Ah, Carlotta, nice to hear from you," he said. "How are you enjoying things?"

I informed him that I was already on the way

---

teeny-weeny – winzig

home and would be arriving at 14:58. I had the impression he had completely forgotten I'd be coming back this afternoon.

"Yes, of course, how nice," he said in embarrassment. "Look, I admit it. It completely slipped my mind you were coming home today. There was so much to do in the office, and the man who lives above Jenny let the bath overflow. You can imagine how her flat looked. But at least the worst has been cleared up and soon ..."

"Listen, can you collect us at 14:58 please?" I interrupted him.

"What do you mean, 'us'?"

"Natascha and me, of course. Who else?"

I heard Dad gulp.

"Tell me, does that mean things are all right between you two?"

"Hello, hello, I can't understand what you're saying any more," I shouted into the phone and then hung up. I didn't want to answer Dad's last question.

When Dad saw Natascha at the station in her pink tracksuit, she could play the artist as much as she wanted, for him it would all be over. I was sure of that.

On the way back to the compartment I had to go past Dad's ex (as I was already calling her) again. She was still standing at the window gazing out. When she saw me, she reached into her trouser pocket and pulled out an envelope. 'Does she want to **blackmail** me?' went through my

---

to blackmail – erpressen

head. At first I just wanted to continue on my way, but then I was curious.

"Carlotta, dear," she said, smiling at me, "it's very difficult to get hold of you. I've been carrying this envelope around with me for ages. Will you take it at last?"

I nodded and stuck out my hand. She handed me a rather **crumpled** envelope on which someone had written in large letters: *For Carlotta. Personal!!*

"Carlotta," called Anke from further back. "Are you coming? We want to play cards."

"I'll be there soon. Give me a couple of minutes," I called and went to look for an empty compartment. I somehow had the feeling I wanted to be alone when I opened the letter.

At the very end of the train I found a carriage with no one in it. Just to make sure, I asked the guard if this part of the train was going to be uncoupled.

"Where did you get that ridiculous idea from?" asked the man in amazement.

I didn't reply. I opened the door to a compartment and closed it carefully behind me. I drew the curtains to the corridor and sat down. My heart was pounding and my fingers were **trembling** slightly as I opened the letter. A piece of lined paper from a school exercise book fluttered to the floor. I picked it up and read: *If you like Jannis, open the second envelope. If not, throw it away and forget the whole thing. Olli.*

---

crumpled – zerknittert;
to tremble – zittern

There really was a second, carefully folded envelope in the first one, which was why the letter was so thick. I opened it cautiously. Now my heart was pounding fit to burst.

I'm Jannis's best friend and I think I **owe** *him this letter. Do you know that he's incredibly in love with you? He just doesn't have the courage to tell you because he's afraid you might not like him so much. But I* **suspect** *you like him, too. Here's his telephone number. But please don't tell him I wrote to you.*

PS: could you send me the address of the blonde some time? I think her name's Anke. Thanks!

I could feel the tears welling up in my eyes. I had to read the sentence over and over again: *Do you know that he's incredibly in love with you?*

I was crying and laughing at the same time. Olli, thank you, thank you. Of course I'll send you Anke's address, and her shoe size and whatever else you want. I was simply overjoyed and was about to kiss the letter when the guard opened the door and eyed me suspiciously. "Is everything all right with you?" he asked.

"Yes," I said. "Everything's all right now. Really. I'm fine. I'm doing great."

"Well then," said the man, "go on back to the front. I think they're looking for you."

"We thought you'd got off the train without reporting to Danni," said Stefanie. Natascha was

---

to owe – schulden;
to suspect – vermuten

terribly worried about you. She muttered something about a letter and ..."

"What letter?" asked Anke as she dealt the cards. "Anything special?"

"No," I said, "Not really. But now I'm looking forward to being back home, too."

"I'll call Jannis and talk to him, call Jannis and talk to him," sang the carriage wheels, and I smiled with happiness, and Anke put down an ace and said I'd never played so badly.

Perhaps the magic stone had worked after all. If Natascha hadn't given me the letter – well, it didn't **bear** thinking about. Supposing she'd put her tracksuit in the washing machine back home and washed the letter, too. The **ink** would have run, and I wouldn't have known a thing, not a thing.

"Hey, stop making such a horrified face," I heard Anke saying. "It's your own fault if you lose all the time. You're playing as if you'd never *seen* a pack of cards before."

"Yes," I said and tried to concentrate, but it was pointless. I just kept on thinking about phoning Jannis that evening.

Dad would be surprised when I disappeared into my room straight away with the telephone, but he had Natascha and perhaps he'd even be pleased if I wasn't around and ...

No, he'd be alone, of course. The game was up for Natascha in her pink tracksuit. Dad's love would never go that far.

---

to bear – ertragen;
ink – Tinte

I got up, carelessly laying down my cards, mumbled something about needing to go to the loo and ran to the toilet. Right now I needed a place where I could think in peace and quiet.

If the thing with Natascha fell apart, Dad would have more time, of course, for me as well. He'd probably even be interested in who I was making long-distance calls to for hours ... I sighed. Actually, Natascha wasn't so bad. She knew how to have fun, had made the school trip possible, hadn't snapped at me, even though I'd been pretty mean sometimes, and had given me the letter from Olli that was going to change my life.

I looked at myself critically in the mirror. I'm not a child any more, I thought, so I can't act childishly either. Even towards Natascha. When I thought about my plan to show her up, I felt quite sick. "Childish and mean," I said to myself softly. "It was childish and mean and doesn't reflect what you really are."

I looked at my watch. Half past two. If I didn't do something, Natascha would be making a complete disgrace of herself in 28 minutes. Dad would probably pretend not to know her any more. And in front of everyone! No, I had to do something, and do it quickly and inconspicuously.

For the hundredth time that day I ran along the corridor and found Natascha in the compartment with Danni, who had woken up in the meantime.

"Hello," I said, trying to keep my voice sounding harmless. "Can I sit with you for a bit?"

Danni looked at me mistrustfully. "You haven't

got some kind of surprise for us? Your friend hasn't got off by accident at the previous stop? No?"

"No, of course not," I said. "I just don't feel like playing cards any more and so ..."

Mr Dannitzki realised we were arriving in 20 minutes and said he wanted to have a quick cup of coffee. "My wife is against me drinking coffee or tea after half past one," he explained. "She says it makes it difficult to go to sleep. This is my last chance."

"But of course," said Natascha. "Go and have your coffee."

Then it was just the two of us in the compartment. Only 17 minutes; I had to hurry. At first I wanted to give her some kind of story, but then I decided to be honest. "Natascha," I began, "I have to tell you something."

She looked at me expectantly. "Yes?"

"My father hates tracksuits. He particularly dislikes pink tracksuits. So, I mean, perhaps you should ..."

At first she stared at me in disbelief, and I had the feeling she was about to burst into laughter. But I was wrong.

"You mean I should wear a sweater over it," she asked. "The black one, for example."

I shook my head. If you're going to do something, you might as well do it properly. "No, the skirt and jacket you had on in the museum. The blue one with the stripes. You know the one I mean."

"She nodded. "Of course, I only have the one. But it's a bit too light, really. You know, my **land-**

lord still hasn't turned the heating on despite the low temperatures, and I'll freeze to death at home in just a skirt and jacket."

"You ... you could come with us," I suggested after a short hesitation. "Dad can **light** the **stove**, then you won't freeze."

"Yes, that wouldn't be too bad," said Natascha slowly. "Are you sure you don't mind? Honestly?"

"As long as you don't cook noodles with chocolate sauce," I said.

"All right, I won't," she said, winking at me. "But now I have to hurry up and get changed."

Of course Dad came to the station too late. Natascha and I sat on the platform talking, almost as if we were friends.

"I think it was right you came on the trip with us," I said because I still had a guilty conscience. I had been pretty impossible after all.

"Your father talked me into it," Natascha admitted. "I didn't want to go at all. The noodles with chocolate sauce probably gave me such a shock that I ..."

"It wasn't your idea with the school trip?" I interrupted. "But Dad pretended as if you really wanted to go."

"And to me he pretended that you really wanted me to come. I thought you were too shy to tell me yourself, and your father ..."

---

landlord – Vermieter;
to light – anzünden;
stove – Heizofen

"I almost suspect my father was glad to get rid of us for a while. Perhaps that's why he's so late," I laughed. But in reality I didn't feel like laughing at all. What if he already had another new girlfriend, just when I was getting on so well with Natascha!

At last Dad ran up. He pretended it was normal to see the two of us sitting next to each other on a suitcase. "Hurry up, I'm in a no-parking zone," he called. "There wasn't a parking place for miles around as usual."

"I didn't hear from you the whole time," he said when he had to stop at a red light. He turned around to me in the back. "Not even a postcard ..."

For a moment I thought **frantically** about what to say, but Natascha just laughed and said she had written for both of us. Hadn't Dad deciphered the **scrawl** at the edge of her card as *Love from Carlotta*?

Dad drummed his fingers on the steering wheel. "I didn't get any post from you. Probably the card got lost. The incompetence everywhere. Last month in the company we had ..."

The lights changed to green and he put his foot down.

Natascha put her hand on his arm. "Cards don't get lost that easily. Just wait. Perhaps it'll come tomorrow."

But this card would never come, I knew that

---

frantic – verzweifelt;
scrawl – Gekritzel

for sure. What had Natascha been thinking of, sending Dad my love?

Dad pulled up in front of the garden gate. "Everybody out!" he called in a good mood. "What's up, Carlotta? You're pulling a funny face."

"Oh, nothing," I said, eying Natascha unobtrusively. What had Danni said? She was an outstanding actress. The message on the card would have made Dad think everything was fine and ...

At that moment Natascha turned around to me and smiled.

All right, I thought, we both did a bit of play-acting. And anyway, I didn't want any long discussions right now; I wanted to get to the phone as quickly as possible. And while I was about it, perhaps I could ask Jannis about the Walkman that was sent on to them.

But first we had coffee and ate the cake Dad had bought at the bakery.

"I'm going to my room to unpack," I said after a while. "By the way, where's the phone?"

"I think it's upstairs," said Dad. "In the hall, in the bathroom, you'll find it."

Only five minutes and I'll be talking to Jannis, I thought. I looked in the hall, in the bathroom. I looked for the telephone in all the rooms upstairs, but it was nowhere to be seen. For two seconds I **got into a temper** because everything was going wrong yet again, but then I reminded

---

to get into a temper – sich aufregen

myself I wasn't going to be childish any more and went downstairs to look there.

Through the half-open door I could hear Dad's voice. "Isn't it too cold in that thin skirt and jacket? It's the end of March, but it still feels like winter. Put on the tracksuit I gave you for Christmas. The pink one, it's nice and cosy."

For a moment I shut my eyes. But then I had to grin. Dad really seemed to have changed since he'd met Natascha. Actually, I wanted to make some comment about it, but then I found the telephone on the hall cupboard.

"Everything all right?" asked Dad from the living room.

"Yes," I called back. "Everything's fine now!"

I ran to my room with the phone in my hand.

Von Zimmermann & Zimmermann
u. a. ebenfalls bei Thienemann erschienen:

Mathe, Stress & Liebeskummer
Liebe, Chaos, Klassenfahrt
Küsse, Krisen, große Ferien
Schule, Frust & große Liebe
Küsse, Chaos, Feriencamp
Freche Mädchen – freche Ferien
Maths, Stress and a Lovesick Heart
School, Trouble & True Love

Zimmermann & Zimmermann:
School Trip, Love & Trouble
Aus dem Deutschen von Michael Turnbull
ISBN 978 3 522 18039 9

Reihengestaltung: Birgit Schössow
Einbandillustration und -typografie: Birgit Schössow
Texttypografie: Marlis Killermann
Schrift: Candida und Klepto
Satz: KCS GmbH, Buchholz/Hamburg
Reproduktion: Medienfabrik, Möglingen
Druck und Bindung: Friedrich Pustet, Regensburg

6 5 4 3 2°   08 09 10 11

www.thienemann.de
www.frechemaedchen.de